M000189261

Dealing with Dysfunction

Dealing with Dysfunction

A Book for University Leaders

Richard T. Castallo

ROWMAN & LITTLEFIELD
Lanham • Boulder • New York • London

Published by Rowman & Littlefield
A wholly owned subsidiary of The Rowman & Littlefield Publishing Group, Inc.
4501 Forbes Boulevard, Suite 200, Lanham, Maryland 20706
www.rowman.com

Unit A, Whitacre Mews, 26-34 Stannary Street, London SE11 4AB

Copyright © 2017 by Richard T. Castallo

All rights reserved. No part of this book may be reproduced in any form or by any electronic or mechanical means, including information storage and retrieval systems, without written permission from the publisher, except by a reviewer who may quote passages in a review.

British Library Cataloguing in Publication Information Available

Library of Congress Cataloging-in-Publication Data

Names: Castallo, Richard T., 1950- author.
Title: Dealing with dysfunction : a book for university leaders / Richard T. Castallo.
Description: Lanham : Rowman & Littlefield, [2017]
Identifiers: LCCN 2017009256 (print) | LCCN 2017026880 (ebook) | ISBN 9781475834833 (Electronic) | ISBN 9781475834819 (cloth : alk. paper) | ISBN 9781475834826 (pbk. : alk. paper)
Subjects: LCSH: Universities and colleges--Departments. | College teachers--Professional relationships. | Universities and colleges--Administration. | Educational leadership.
Classification: LCC LB2360.2 (ebook) | LCC LB2360.2 .C37 2017 (print) | DDC 371.10082--dc23
LC record available at https://lccn.loc.gov/2017009256

∞ ™ The paper used in this publication meets the minimum requirements of American National Standard for Information Sciences Permanence of Paper for Printed Library Materials, ANSI/NISO Z39.48-1992.

Printed in the United States of America

To the best leaders I know: Logan, Max, Olivia, and Sydney.
Thank you for being great examples.

Contents

Acknowledgments

I have been blessed with the opportunity to work with a wealth of great leaders in education. These include a number of central office administrators, chairs, deans, provosts, and presidents in higher education.

Nothing is more interesting to participate in than the calls, lunches, and occasional drinks they shared with me as they told their stories.

A few years ago I made a presentation to a leadership training program for chairs and deans. Harry Hellenbrand, the highly respected Provost at CSU Northridge, made the statement in his introduction that department chairs had the toughest job in higher education. Well said. I placed that quote in the text somewhere—thank you, Harry.

Having been a school principal, as well as a chair, I realized he was absolutely correct. It is the middle managers in education that provide the glue to our educational organizations. Provosts, presidents, and others in central offices tend to come and go. The men and women in the middle of the organizational ladder receive much less of the recognition, yet they are the ones that are relied upon to provide an understanding of our history and the know-how to reach our desired future.

I thank the many wonderful chairs that I have had the opportunity to serve with, and the handful of exceptional deans, provosts, and presidents that provided me with the stories I have been able to share here.

I particularly want to thank my friends and colleagues, Bonnie Ericson, Bev Cabello, and Bill Silky, for their reviews and suggestions.

Introduction

In most universities, departments are psychologically self-sustaining. Professors are given more latitude than in almost any other vocation in order to explore work that is of interest to them. Many concentrate on research and writing. Some focus on providing exciting learning opportunities for their students. Hours are typically flexible, with chunks of time available during lengthy break periods to travel and explore and meet with others in their fields. In addition to local support, a large number of institutions provide opportunities to gain external funding for in-depth study of unique ideas.

Having peers in the department to talk with about these efforts is one of the best features of being a university faculty member. Most of these opportunities do not exist at the same level in the corporate world. Professors get to seek out colleagues within their departments with whom they can share ideas, draft proposals, and initiate research ideas. This is one of the best things about the profession, and when it no longer exists, it is one of the greatest losses.

The department and faculty members described in this book are fictional. However, the characters that are introduced came about as a result of interviews with colleagues in higher education along with the experiences of the author.

The first chapter of the book introduces a long-term professor who is employed within a dysfunctional Secondary Education Department. The professor was chair of the department in the past and has been approached by colleagues and the university's dean to see if he would be willing to return to the chair position. His primary role, if he is willing to accept their request, is to help the department get back to the point where members can work together smoothly to provide quality education to its students.

THE COMMITTED, THE RELUCTANTS, AND THE RESISTORS

As you consider your colleagues in the department, you see them falling primarily into one of three categories: Committed, Reluctants, and Resistors.

The *Committed* faculty consists of members that are typically above-average instructors who understand that success is the result of faculty, staff, and administration working toward common goals through compromise and negotiation. They are student oriented. They realize that not everyone can have his or her own way on every issue. They willingly serve on committees, volunteer to do their share of the work in order to accomplish departmental goals, and regularly show up and participate in activities like honors convocations and graduation. Most are well-liked by students; all are well-respected by students.

The *Reluctants* are a second group within the department. These people have tried to stay out of the dissension that has occurred. Some are new faculty who feel caught in the middle, between the Resistors and school leaders. They fear retribution by Resistors if they are seen as supportive of administration. They are also afraid that if they do too good a job teaching or with their research they might be a threat to Resistors. As a result, they often tend to hold back. They are concerned that if they volunteer to support department initiatives they will be the target of derision by Resistors who may be on committees when they are being considered for reappointment, tenure, and other opportunities that might arise.

Not all Reluctants are nontenured. Some veteran department members are just psychologically exhausted by the negativism that has surfaced in the last few years. They are deeply disappointed that the role of department chair has changed almost every year because of the instability it has caused, and as a result, faculty members cannot work together cooperatively. They are saddened that some colleagues in the department are critical of fellow faculty and administrators in public forums where they are overheard by students as well as other professionals in the university. Just living with these people on a day-to-day basis is uncomfortable, and the idea of actually trying to work with them to accomplish any goals is considered unlikely.

The department has suffered the last few years as a result of splintering within the faculty. As a result, the third group that you have identified within the faculty is the *Resistors*. These people have little trust in the administration. Some are poor instructors; some are resentful because they believe that other colleagues have been given opportunities that they have not been provided. Some are simply self-centered and do not want to meet the expectations of the university in terms of teaching, research, and contributions to the university and community.

Several of the Resistors have found and support each other. While their reasons for being Resistors vary, their interest in being combative and regularly trying to usurp and challenge authority provides them with some common interests.

Following a discussion on the structure of leadership in different organizations, and the complex role of department chairs, you will become more familiar with the main character of this story as he volunteers to return to the role of chair in his department. He will work with his dean to develop a plan of action to address the many concerns that have arisen in hopes of developing a more cohesive and collaborative department.

The following chapters will present six different department members as case studies, and their behaviors and experiences at various times during the chair's first year in his return to the position will be detailed. These cases will involve individuals from all three of the categories described above: Resistors, Reluctants, and Committed faculty.

You will see that no one falls solely into one of these categories. As you read and get to know them you will see that their behaviors are typically situational and often cross over into a neighboring category as the situation they are involved in develops.

CHAIR AND DEAN

You will view the cases from the chair's perspective and will get to hear what the chair learns as information comes to him in the course of each one. You will be privy to the highlights of discussions he has with faculty members, as well as the dean and the provost in one case.

The chair's experience in the department is often intense and trying. When viewing some of these cases with him, you will get a personal view of what he did and why he did it. You will also hear from the dean and understand the importance of the relationship between deans and chairs if colleges are to operate successfully.

Finally, you will get to listen in on a conversation between the dean and chair several years after they have completed their terms at the university. As you hear what they have to say, you will gain an idea of what they believe was helpful and successful, what they would do differently if placed in similar circumstances, and their conclusions about dealing with challenging faculty members in higher education settings.

As the story unfolds, the dean has determined that the department is at a point of no return in its present state. She has decided that every reasonable effort should be made to reconcile the problems that exist over the next year. If at that point reasonable progress has not been made, she believes that some hard decisions must take place.

At this time, the first step is to remove as many of the distractions as possible. This may include events, programs, and even personnel. The dean's job here is to first determine what is negotiable and what is non-negotiable. The dean's second job is to determine how to solve each problem.

THE AXIS OF NEGATIVE BEHAVIORS

As you listen in on some of the conversations that take place between the dean and the chair, you will hear them refer to the "Axis of Negative

Behaviors." Both the dean and chair have academic backgrounds and lengthy experiences in behavioral sciences and leadership. Based on their observations of what is occurring in the dysfunctional department, they witness people and behaviors generally falling into one of three categories: Passive, Passive-Aggressive, and Aggressive.

The kinds of negative behaviors they have observed in each of these situations include the following:

PASSIVE	*PASSIVE-AGGRESSIVE*	*AGGRESSIVE*
Absences and lateness to classes and meetings	Ignoring specific responsibilities (e.g., calling meetings, maintaining office hours)	Yelling, screaming
Falling behind on work	Quietly undermining requests	Bullying others
Delay in responding	Excessive sarcasm	Surreptitious behaviors (e.g., unsigned criticisms on bulletin boards)
Silent treatment/avoidant behavior	Poor teaching, supervision	Harassment
Ignoring emails, requests	Requesting special treatment (e.g., classrooms, courses)	Lying
Feigning confusion and misunderstanding of directives and requests	Refusing to talk in meetings	Refusing to meet obligations (e.g., committee work)
Deferring to others	Requiring a union rep at all meetings with chair or dean	Discriminatory practices

As the dean and chair discuss some of the individuals in the case studies presented in chapters 7 through 12, regular references will be made to the Axis.

THE SETTING

The dean, with the support of the provost, has been open with the department regarding their perceptions of its status and where it might head in the future. Efforts that have been made up to this point have included activities such as individual interviews with faculty, the use of outside consultants, offers to provide for individual counseling, as well as group discussions with faculty and staff.

Unfortunately, none of these efforts have brought the group back together. If things do not improve, the department has been put on notice that they may no longer function in a traditional mode but instead will operate under the supervision of the dean's office. She or her designee will make virtually all major decisions that are not covered by contract or legislation. Thus, decision making related to the structure of the department, communications, subcommittees, assignments, and organization will be reviewed and will operate under the approval of the dean.

FACULTY

The department has seventeen full-time faculty members. The following individuals will be introduced during the course of the case studies:

Name	Subject	Category	Employment Length
Andrew	Science	Committed Reluctant	17 years, tenured
Anthony	English	Senior Resistor	14 years, tenured
Antoine	Social Science	Aggressive Resistor	19 years, tenured
Bill	Math	Committed	18 years, tenured
Bruce	English	Passive-Aggressive Resistor	12 years, tenured
Jennifer	English	Vulnerable Reluctant	5 years, nontenured
Marianne	English	Resistor	16 years, tenured
Mary	Science	Passive Resistor	9 years, tenured
Ronald	Science	Committed	22 years, tenured
Sandy	Social Science	Committed Reluctant	14 years, tenured

ONE

Opportunity?

"We should treat each other the same way we tell our student teachers to treat their first graders"

—Education professor

Imagine this: You are a tenured college professor. Consequently, you have a record of success in your profession. You get to choose areas of study that are of interest to you and develop questions that you want to research. For the most part, no one tells you what you can research, when you can do it, or how you will go about doing it. You also have the ability to consult with outside groups and organizations and make additional money. In some cases, this can be for rather impressive amounts.

While you are blessed with a work schedule that has a good deal of flexibility, you are well aware that the time you spend on campus fulfilling university duties, along with time researching and planning, calls for you to put in more than the average 40-hour work week. On some days, you may work from 6:00 a.m. until noon, attend an afternoon meeting, and then put in time later in the day after your kids have been fed. Some of your colleagues schedule their time so that they are working in the evening after dinner and late into the night; others like to crunch their writing into the weekends when their phones are not ringing; and many find time sitting on airplanes to be opportune. That is the beauty of the job. The demands are high, but you have a good deal of personal choice in what you do and how you go about doing it.

Your work also allows you to be highly independent—in other words, you do a lot of your own research—and while you may use graduate assistants, there is no need to physically supervise them daily. And although your work may require some contact with other parties, you can usually make those contacts through your own scheduled meetings and

1

phone calls. However, because you love what you do, it really is not work.

Many would agree that it is one of the best jobs in the world. In addition to what is described above, you get to work with a lot of young people along with a sprinkling of individuals of all ages. One thing they have in common is that they have invested their time as well as their money to learn from you. They are working to gain the skills and knowledge that will carry them on to the next stage of their lives, and as a result, most are highly motivated and hungry. What could be better?

And so, one day in late spring, you are leaving a department faculty meeting of your peers. These meetings occur every month or so. They usually last two to three hours and provide the faculty with the chance to talk about how the department is working, the status of enrollments, the latest edicts from the dean's office and central administration, and other sundry and random topics. They also provide the chance to socialize, exchange updates on research efforts, and share more personal anecdotes involving kids, health, who is taking what job, who is planning to retire, and who is likely to win the Super Bowl this year.

However, this day is different. The meeting is scheduled to end at noon. The dean has requested a spot on the agenda at 11:30. She has indicated that she wants to talk about the state of the department. This is not a surprise to anyone. In recent years a lot of bickering has occurred. People have splintered off into multiple small groups, and some of them have behaved in destructive ways toward peers in the department.

Interventions to stop these behaviors have occurred, with outsiders providing organizational development (OD) efforts through surveys, as well as individual, small group, and departmental discussions.

Some reorganization of programs and committees within the department has occurred, and in a few cases disciplinary actions have been necessary, all to no avail. The climate is still toxic. The provost has met with the department and threatened the possibility of total dissolution, with a plan to reassign individuals to other departments if matters do not improve. However, even with all this, the sniping has continued.

At the appointed time, the dean enters the paneled conference room used for faculty meetings. She shares her perceptions of the department and reviews all of the efforts that have been made thus far. She notes her disappointment in the faculty's failure to work through the problems that have arisen. She puts the faculty on notice that she plans to appoint a new chair to serve over the next year. If at that time significant progress is not made, she will be providing the provost with a report on the status of the department, and the next stage may actually involve steps toward dissolution of the department.

Following the dean's visit, two of your colleagues catch you in the hallway and say they need to talk to you. "Let's do lunch," one suggests. You agree, and after you have dropped your meeting notes and laptop in your office, you head for the parking lot to meet up with your friends and go to lunch.

Once you get there and the waitress takes your order, they share why they have asked you to come: "We are in crisis. While a couple of senior professors have remained pretty independent, almost everyone in the department is seen as belonging to one group or another. Obviously, what we've gone through, and where we are at, is not improving. You were chair years ago and resigned the position on your own. You seem to be the only one in the department that would not only have the skills to take the job, but also not be seen as tightly aligned with any one group. We really need you to consider coming back to the chair position."

"Oh Lord," you think to yourself. "This isn't what I was expecting." Yes, the department is a mess. But what the heck, you have the flexibility to come and go and conduct your research and writing as you please. Nobody bothers you, and while some faculty seems to thrive on the drama that is going on, it is something you have avoided. At the same time, there is one awful truth that you also know is front and center: Students are not getting served as well as they should.

Most faculty members, even some of the bitter and nasty ones, are pretty good about taking their teaching seriously. However, everyone knows that there are a couple that are just plain bad instructors that also happen to be bad colleagues. Whether they do not have the skills to be effective, or just do not want to be effective, you are not sure. But you were not involved in hiring them and have not been involved in their supervision. As a result, you have been able to avoid them for the most part.

However, as you are also well aware, there are no secrets in a college department. As a mentor once told you, "If you want to keep a secret from a faculty, make sure it's between you and a dead man!" Everyone knows who the poor instructors are. Everyone knows who is acting un-professional. The students talk to other professors. You overhear conver-sations in your classes. You sit on committees with some of these faculty and see who works hard to avoid taking responsibilities, or misses meet-ings, or shows up late, or does not prepare for classes. It is obvious, and unfortunately, it is known throughout the greater college and university.

Everyone is aware of some version of what is going on. In some cases, what they have learned is accurate, but in many other cases, it is highly inaccurate, making the perceptions even worse than reality. Unfortunate-ly, the system is built in such a way that ineffective and negative people are protected beyond what some might find reasonable. As a result, those who have integrity and a work ethic continue to take on responsibilities so that students are served properly, while many of their colleagues re-fuse to share in these responsibilities.

You let your friends know that you are surprised and flattered to be asked to take on this challenge. You also let them know you need a few days to talk with your spouse and think about it.

THE CONVERSATION

"Are you out of your mind?" your wife asks you. The pasta and wine were as tasty as ever. Midway through the meal, when your spouse asks you how school was today, you share the conversation that took place. "You have got to be crazy!" she says with a laugh.

She reminds you that after you had served as department chair for three years and then returned to the professorship, you vowed you would never do it again. She reminds you of how much you love being able to travel and write and conduct research in the summer, how you appreciate being able to come home and pay no attention to your email after supper, how much you enjoy being able to sleep late any time you want to and then spend a leisurely hour at the coffee shop having a cappuccino and reading the *Times*.

You sit there, nodding in agreement. And yet, there is this nagging conversation going on in your head. You were brought up in a home where it was ingrained that you owed your employer your best. Your mom was a teacher, and it was always clear that you are there to serve students. You watched her, year after year, bring work home virtually every night and weekend and correct papers, write notes, call parents, and participate in professional development all because it was going to help children in the end.

Damn. This should be an easy decision . . . but it's not. You get a call the next morning and the dean's administrative assistant asks if you can come up for a cup of coffee. Actually, when the dean's administrative assistant "asks," she is telling you that you will be coming up for a cup of coffee. And so you graciously "accept" the offer, and at 10:00 a.m. you meet with the dean.

Skilled college administration is based on the art of persuasion. Warren Bennis described getting agreement from college faculty as like "Trying to herd cats." College faculty contains the most highly educated union in the world. They take pride in their diversity of thought as well as behavior. The protections of labor unions provide them the freedom to pretty much tell anyone to go to hell as long as it is done with a modicum of savvy. And many do.

However, most college faculties are truly dedicated to their students, their disciplines, and their schools. Because of this, the informal organization dictates a number of unspoken, but understood, truths:

1. Our primary purpose is to serve students.

2. We have a responsibility to contribute to our disciplines as scholars.
3. We will give our time to perpetuate the values of the institution.
4. We respect academic freedom.
5. While we work under the provisions outlined in contracts, we realize that both labor and management have to interpret contract provisions loosely at times, with each side giving and taking in order to make things work.

While the above are not typical topics of conversation, it is understood that they are a pretty common part of the unspoken culture that new faculty learn about when they enter a department.

It is 10:00 a.m. on the nose when you get to the dean's office. The administrative assistant, like most dean's assistants, is a highly skilled and competent part of the college. She coordinates with other professionals in the office, supervises the student workers, handles her boss's complicated and busy schedule, answers questions knowingly, and is a superior manager of conflict resolution. She welcomes you with a smile, steps into the dean's office to let her know you have arrived, and ushers you in.

You get the big smile and handshake. "Hey, how are you doing? How did your year go?" You exchange pleasantries and get caught up on each other's activities. Sitting across from you, legs crossed, a beaming smile on her face, she shares, "I have a great opportunity for you." That's when you know, right away, you're in trouble!

Once the greeting is complete, she shares that she is truly concerned with the state of the department. She recaps much of what you already know—efforts to have outsiders come in and do development with the faculty have been fruitless, concerns rising to her level are increasing as a result of complaints from both students and parents, and the employment of outside chairs has not worked out. As a result, you are the one person who is relatively well accepted by all department members, and she would really like you to consider taking leadership and bringing sanity back.

She immediately points out the need to act with urgency. The efforts made thus far have not been effective, and she has come to the conclusion that the behaviors of several faculty need to be addressed fairly but firmly. She specifically addresses at the outset the need for a commitment, by her and by you, to engage in uncomfortable conversations with peers. She stresses that in order for any change to occur in the department, both of you will likely be involved in confrontational, and not always comfortable, conversations with faculty and staff.

These conversations, she explains, are not easy and do imply conflict, conflict that must at all times be respectful but at the same time assertive in reinforcing goals for the department. The dean also indicates that documenting these conversations, and their outcomes, is almost as important as having the conversations in the first place. Without clear delineation of expectations, by both of you, no significant change will likely result or take place in the department. You can immediately tell by the manner in which she brings this topic up that the dean is evaluating whether or not you are up to this part of the assignment.

You take a deep breath and reflect on this interaction. There is nothing the dean has shared that you do not know. There are no new revelations here, and you are conscious of the fact that if you do not do this, there is not a real clear Plan B that appears to be workable. You have given this some thought since being approached by your colleagues in the department and after speaking with your spouse who, after letting you know you must be out of your mind, also told you to do what you think you need to and you would have her support.

You tell the dean, with more than a little trepidation, that you will take the job. However, before leaving the dean's office, you let her know that while you are willing, you want a few days to put together an action plan that you will present to her. You make it clear that you have given this some thought and if you take this responsibility on, you need to know that you will have support to do it the way that you think it needs to be done. You share that if your plan of action seems reasonable to her, then you are willing to move forward. Likewise, if it does not appear to be acceptable, you will be glad to stay in your present position with no hard feelings.

The dean agrees to your request.

Learnings

1. Unlike any other organization, well-functioning colleges and universities are run by the workers (faculty), and the role of administration is to support them in that effort. Commensurate with that role is the responsibility of faculty to be fair, conscientious, and committed to the growth of students.
2. There will always be at least a handful of people who do not subscribe to Learning #1.

Reflections

1. One of the first tests of leadership involves the courage of the leader to "fail forward." In other words, to develop a level of comfort while trying out a variety of interventions, without the associated anxiety of worrying about whether or not the choice selected is always the right one. A strong level of trust between the dean and the chair is necessary to allow this to happen.

2. An associated element of leadership involves the ability to check one's ego at the door; this requires recognizing when there is not a match between the person and the task, and hence the comment that you will stay in your present position if there is not a goodness of fit between your style and skills and the task at hand.

3. Third, whether going into a position as a present member of the staff or from the outside, having a clear understanding of job expectations and responsibilities is critical to later success.

TWO

A Bottle of Wine and a Lot of Rumination

"How do you work with someone when you are constantly looking over your shoulder?"

—Psychology professor

Since you are a college professor, you do what college professors do when faced with a problem to solve—you approach it as a research problem to be answered. Research typically starts with a question. In this case: How do you make a disparate group of individuals cohesive? This seems to be a good start. And before making a trip into any literature, you think about the potential positives as well as the concerns associated with the department (you will not allow yourself to think in terms of "negatives" as you ponder this). Your list seems to fall into three categories: one involves the university; the second, the college; and the third includes the department and its members.

First, colleagues in the university are sorely, and sadly, aware of the problems that exist. The good news is that there is widespread support from the *Power Tower* (president, provost, personnel offices, and other interested parties) to see changes occur that will benefit students and contributing members of the faculty and staff. Concerns include the fact that some of the behaviors that have occurred up to this point have been an embarrassment.

There have been student and parent complaints about some of the teaching, supervision, and advising that have occurred (or failed to occur in some instances). Peers in the university make comments about the department's very public dysfunction. Many have witnessed faculty and staff making demeaning and critical remarks about colleagues when attending meetings and other functions.

9

Awareness of what is occurring at the college level shows that this dysfunction is not dissimilar to the larger university. Faculty from neighboring departments know their secondary education colleagues well since they interact so often in committees and their offices are all within the same four floors of the building. The good news is that, overall, students are receiving a good education. Evaluations by graduating students are typically positive, and most report that they feel prepared to take on positions of responsibility once they leave. Surveys that are strongly critical are usually aimed at just a couple of people.

Second, the dean has a lot at stake. She has worked with the provost to provide opportunities for the department to move forward effectively. This has included outside consultants, changes in leadership, counseling opportunities, and responses, where possible, to individual requests. While these have not had much success, no one can criticize her willingness to recognize the situation and the efforts she has made to try to fix it. You also recognize that placing you in the chair position would be a final effort, and the dean and provost are serious about total dissolution of the department if something does not happen now.

Finally, at the individual department level, a number of good things are taking place. Some of the best teachers in the college can be found within the department. Most of the faculty is dedicated to the students and to providing them an excellent education. However, on an interpersonal level, things are a disaster.

As you drink your glass of wine and reflect on the personal and professional mix, you realize that most of the unhappy and unproductive teachers that you have known in your career are also unhappy people. How often do you see someone who whines and complains in the school hallway become joyous and ebullient when you run into them at the mall or in a local restaurant? However, in this situation, you truly do have a real mix, each of which will now be described in turn.

Group A, the *Committed*, is the group of faculty who sincerely like interacting with students, love teaching, are good colleagues, and volunteer to help with advising, graduation ceremonies, chairing committees, and the myriad other duties expected of effective college professors. They want the department to remain healthy and productive, often to their own detriment when it comes to taking on the responsibilities and tasks of others.

This group is committed to the success of the department, the college, and the university on a macro level. Student success is the ultimate driver of their work, and they collectively take pride in the achievements of their students. In short, this group is self-motivated and will always go the extra mile in pursuit of success.

Then there is Group B, the *Reluctants*. Overall, this group could be described as taking a wait-and-see approach to their work. They are typically good instructors who quietly meet their responsibilities. They do not approve of the behavior of some of their colleagues, but they do not want to get involved in the mire. Consequently, they usually avoid making any comments when they are in groups with a mix of faculty, and they are careful not to take sides in discussions that might indicate their agreement with one group or another. In some cases, these members do not want to get caught up in the conflict. In others, they feel insecure and vulnerable.

Finally, Group C, the *Resistors*, is made up of those whose performance as instructors, colleagues, and professionals often leaves much to be desired in one or more of these areas. Overall, this group is comprised of faculty who are not vested in the mission and goals of the department, college, or university. If you try to come up with positives for this group, you struggle. When you consider potential concerns, you can think of several: As instructors, some of them are actually good with students in the classroom; however, when you review the poorest evaluations given by students, semester after semester, they invariably come from some of the Resistors. Further, the Resistors will make every excuse to avoid teaching more challenging courses. They would prefer that someone else, including adjunct faculty, take on classes that are more demanding.

Complaints include failure to respond to student work, or handing it back without comments or suggestions. The only committees they participate in are those that are mandatory. When they do participate, they refuse to respond or provide only minimal effort. Their classes are often cut short, and online courses are used as a matter of personal convenience for the instructor rather than a learning opportunity for the students.

They never show up for college events hosted by administration, come to hear guest speakers, attend graduation, or get involved in the other social and professional activities that are part of the fabric of most institutions of higher learning. When efforts to find common ground that would help their department move forward have been made, they give them lip service but take no responsibility for the present state of the department, nor do they show a willingness to change.

This handful of people, though relatively small, is so toxic that they have infected the entire department, resulting in the reputation that has become established. Unfortunately, for this department a tipping point has been reached, since several faculty have come together at one time, like a perfect storm, and behaved in this way. The result has been a disaster for the entire department and college.

Having been involved in leadership over a number of years and in several different settings, you realize that contrary to what some might think, you will have to make a concerted effort to deal with people in all three of these groups.

Group A, the Committed, is comprised of your hard chargers and is your most positive group. However, many have gotten discouraged over time as they see colleagues putting in less effort and failing to take on their share of responsibilities. They rightfully feel that they are being "dumped on," and you do not know how long you will be able to maintain their positive support if things continue as they are. And unfortunately, while unionism is positive in many ways, they also see that many of these veteran colleagues are paid more and receive larger raises because of the way the labor contract is negotiated.

Group B, the Reluctants, are the faculty that many administrators think you should focus on. These are people who are on the fence, who may tilt one way or the other with a bit of encouragement. They have not yet been completely lost, and their efforts with students indicate that they are more likely to be brought back into the fold. In reality, a concerted effort to address the needs of these folks is appropriate.

Whether you give more time or less to them is not the issue. What really matters is how entrenched each person is and their willingness to move toward more committed behaviors. What you have learned from your experience in this department is that you are not going to get individuals to consciously declare, "I'm willing to put everything behind me and embrace my fellow colleagues." This may work in certain high-stakes one-on-one marriage counseling situations or possibly some small group settings, but it is not likely to occur in a faculty setting where people have union protection and little fear of losing their positions or status.

Group C, the Resistors, is certainly the most challenging and draining. For whatever reasons, members get more gratification out of not doing their jobs well. Often, they count on chairs and administrators to protect them by fielding complaints from students, parents, and other parties with whom they are involved. To them, putting in a minimum of time and effort trumps service. Behavior for some is passive, with a predilection for staying beneath the radar, while others seemingly get their needs met by taking the opportunity to act out in counterproductive and at times aggressive negative behaviors.

Why someone gets to this point is difficult to understand. And while leaders are obligated to put in a reasonable amount of time and effort gaining insight into what might have caused a faculty member's behavior to go south, it is important for all persons in higher education leadership to remember that the individual is ultimately responsible for his or her own behavior. In these situations, leaders need to be reasonable, and they also need to remember that their primary goal is the education of students and not the resurrection of an adult being paid to do their job.

Without question, simple empathy (helping someone to find counseling, leaves of absence, and other types of support) should be given, but an expectation of cooperation in return is also reasonable.

Having considered all of the above, you determine you will take the position, but before finalizing that decision with the dean, you identify some of the understandings and needs that you have. You let the dean know that you are going to develop an Entry Plan to help guide you as you start in the position. You let her know that you want to ask her for any thoughts and ideas she might have that could be added to the plan. You also let her know that you feel it is important you both agree to the plan and refer to it regularly if you are going to take on this challenge. She agrees with your idea and asks you to get back to her with your plan.

Learnings

1. Change at a department level does not come from a blanket approach but from working with one person at a time.
2. It is important that the values and interests of persons who take on department leadership positions are consistently aligned with the stated values and interests of the department, college, and university.

Reflections

1. Communication—up, down, and sideways—is critical to successful leadership. Without the ongoing give and take of all the people involved in this endeavor, attempts to get the department back on track will be doomed from the start.
2. Although a commitment to wrap-around communication is critical, so is the recognition that all attempts might not prove successful . . . usually for a variety of reasons (some completely out of your control).

THREE

The Plan

Question to faculty member: *What do you need to work in a safe environment?*
Faculty member: *They need to apologize to me.*

Change comes about as a result of a number of factors. Primary among them are beliefs, thoughts, and actions. What we believe directly affects how we think, and ultimately, how we act. These factors do not work in a clear, linear fashion. They are more like geese—one leads while another falls back as the environment varies. They become interchangeable.

You know from reading numerous examples that the rhetoric used in vision and mission statements can drown you in words and phrases that rarely result in any kind of meaningful changes or guidance in how things operate in a school or organization. Consequently, it is critical to keep your guiding belief statements brief, clear, and to the point.

These are statements that you should be able to put on the wall, refer to in conversation, and add to the top of the department's stationery or your business card. Anyone hearing them should know what they mean without lengthy explanation. Ordinarily, these statements would be developed after a great deal of discourse with students, faculty, and staff. However, since faculty has proven itself incapable of civil dialogue, you have decided that you will develop statements for use in your term as chair. After reflecting on the state of the department, you identify three beliefs that you list at the top of your Entry Plan that will help guide your behavior:

Our purpose is to:

1. Responsibly serve our students.
2. Treat all individuals we come in contact with in a civil manner.
3. Build excellent programs.

15

As noted, these statements should be easily understood by anyone in education, but more importantly, they will have special meaning to the faculty members in your college and department because of recent history.

Based on data from students, as well as your own observations, you are well aware that a handful of faculty has provided very substandard teaching. Some faculty members refuse to participate in committees and events to recognize and support students. In some cases, students have been given misinformation or have observed one faculty member "bad-mouthing" another. One faculty member even said he refused to meet with a student to talk about a disagreement since he already knew that he was right and the student was wrong. As far as you are concerned, this has to stop immediately.

Whether at the university or in everyday life, it is never appropriate to be disrespectful toward others. Personal comments made by faculty about others in meetings or hallways are never acceptable. Colleges and universities celebrate their role in society as centers for dissent. This should never change. However, there is a vast difference between social dissent and personal sarcasm, lying, or attacking of others. This is not acceptable at any time, especially in a professional environment.

Finally, a by-product of the first two beliefs is the need to focus on developing excellent, competitive programs that will prepare students in their respective disciplines. Unfortunately, programs serve another purpose for some people: meeting their own needs. For instance, the faculty member who wants to teach all of their courses online, not because it is the best way to reach students in distant locations, or to serve those who have scheduling problems and cannot get to campus, but because doing so allows the faculty member to avoid driving to campus. Or faculty members who believe that certain courses are "theirs" and that their beliefs and opinions are the ones that should be considered in relation to when, how, and where a course is presented in the curriculum.

Likewise, some feel a proprietary right to teach certain more popular courses or groups of students. Unfortunately, these practices you see at the university are also followed in many high schools, where veteran professors and teachers get to teach the most interesting courses, smallest classes, and most highly motivated students, while the "newbies" are given the most difficult and challenging courses and students.

The fact of the matter is that programs in higher education evolve and change. Requirements from credentialing agencies often call for modifications and updating. And while the role of the individual faculty member is very important, it is not the only factor that needs to be considered when looking at what students should know and be able to do as a result of earning a degree in our schools. Unfortunately, there are times that some people forget this.

So you have decided that these three things—(a) commitment to serve students, (b) treating all in a civil manner, and (c) building excellent programs—become the three legs of the stool that will provide the basis for your planning and decision making. In addition to that, you have identified some of the initial steps that need to take place: First, an email needs to be sent to department faculty and staff announcing your appointment by the dean.

STARTING WITH SUPPORT STAFF

Immediately following that communication, you will send an email to each person in the department to share how excited you are to be taking the position, to say how much you look forward to working with everyone, and to invite them to stop in for a cup of coffee to share their thoughts and recommendations on the future of the department. The email will also introduce the aforementioned three tenets of service to students, civility, and building excellent programs that you plan to use to guide you in your role.

Second, since you will be starting the position in the summer, you recognize the extremely important role of office staff in the operation of the department. You realize this group has been close to faculty and in some cases somewhat involved in the dysfunction that has occurred. As a result, you want to hear their recommendations and concerns, as well as give them an idea of your expectations. To do this, you plan to have a luncheon with these personnel within your first few days on the job. The dean should stop in initially to "kick off" the luncheon and then leave and allow you privacy.

In the meeting, staff will be assured that they are welcome to say anything they want to in relation to the agenda and that confidentiality will be honored. You want to let them know that you see protecting and supporting office staff as an important part of your job. Just as you need the support of your boss, you understand that they need your support. They should always expect to be treated civilly, and if anyone, be it a faculty member, student, or administrator, fails to treat them respectfully, they should report the situation to you immediately for handling.

You also make it clear that you are using the time you have as the new chair to assess the total department and that includes personnel, organization, programs, and any other related activities. You may get the question: "Are you planning to change some of our duties?" Or even, "Are you planning to change some of us?"

If so, honesty is critical. You need to let them know that you are looking at everything if in fact that is the case. If not, if you are absolutely sure you will not be displacing or letting personnel go, then assure them of that. In the long run, honesty is important even if it is not what some people might want to hear.

At this time, you want to get a good understanding of the staff's responsibilities and give them a chance to share with you. So you will ask them to respond to a number of requests:

1. To describe their job duties.
2. To describe how the office runs. For example, the role of student workers, whether there are any special needs in terms of equipment, software, or technology.
3. To describe their relationship to faculty: Do they feel supported? Do they feel that anyone tries to take advantage of them or is hostile or demeaning?
4. To identify if there are any major challenges that prevent them from doing their jobs.
5. To describe their view of how students are being served (one of the three tenets).
6. To explain from their perspective whether or not the people they deal with are civil and respectful (the second of the three tenets).
7. To offer ideas on whether there is anything specific you can do to help them.
8. To solicit suggestions that they believe are important to our successfully moving the department in a positive direction.

Likewise, they need to know what you expect of them. Included in this are the following:

1. They should know that you want them to be good listeners to anyone who comes into the office.
2. They should never "lose it" and respond in kind toward anyone who is problematic. It is important that they always keep their tempers in check, and that they report any incidents to you that may need special handling.

In addition, it is absolutely critical that you follow up on any concerns and get back to them with how things worked out. Unfortunately, failure to communicate is a common error in many organizations. Discussions with staff members about contentious incidents often involve hearing, "We told our supervisor but nothing ever happened." Whether something did happen, but the supervisor never got back to them, or nothing happened at all, once people believe that they are not being heard, their trust is quickly lost.

1. When staff is asked to get back to a student, faculty member, or other office in the university on a normal matter, they should do so in a timely manner (hopefully within twenty-four hours during the work week).

2. It is important that no one abuse the system. Computers, telephones, and other office equipment and supplies are for business use, hours of operation should be respected, and personnel procedures should be observed.

Finally, staff need to know how much you appreciate and recognize the important role that they play. They represent the college and university. They are often the first point of contact with students, parents, and other visitors to the campus. If prospective students and parents come to the office at 8:10 a.m. and the door is locked when the sign on the glass says that office hours are from 8:00 a.m. to 4:30 p.m., it leaves an immediate impression, and not a good one. As you will point out to the staff, the first impression that people have will be the result of their visit to your office.

This time with office staff is invaluable and helps lay an important foundation for moving forward. In addition, this initial period is also important for solidifying expectations with the dean. You need to share with the dean that you require her understanding that you will do your best to assure that there will be "no surprises" on your part, and you need the same from her.

SUPPORT FROM THE DEAN

Based on experience, you know that when you end up making a difficult decision, an unhappy faculty or staff member is likely to go around you to the dean to complain. Some department chairs will tell people: "If you have a problem you should come to me first and if you don't like the decision, you can go to the dean." This might be interpreted as you wanting to control all communications and their being restricted from speaking freely. Some will say they feel threatened by you (though not always to your face, but behind your back to others).

The better way of putting it might be to say: "I certainly recognize your right to speak with the dean about any issues; however, if you have a problem, it would be greatly appreciated if you come to me first and we try to work it out. Your call." In fact, documenting this in writing in your first or second communication to the faculty and staff after starting the job is a good idea. Can you be assured that it will not be interpreted negatively? Nope.

Some faculty will come to the conclusion that they are more likely to get the answer they want to a question by going to one person rather than another (kind of like when kids know which parent to go to). Thus, they might decide to go to the dean rather than to their chair. The reverse is also true, and some may go to the chair for a response rather than the dean. Regardless of which person they go to, it is critical that chairs and deans are uniform and consistent. Saying "let me get back to you," and discussing the matter with the dean first is always the best thing to do.

If for some reason a chair's decisions are being reversed on a regular basis, the department chair needs to heed the warning and sharpen his resume. There is only one avenue for the chair. Either your values and decision making are in sync with your dean or they are not. There is little room in between, and ultimately the power rests with the pen.

Be assured, the dean deals with difficult issues on a daily basis. You ask of her is that when faculty do come directly to her office, she redirect them to you if it is appropriate to do so. And in those cases in which she might need to take an action, you ask that she keeps you informed of what occurred so that you can be consistent and supportive as you go forward. The real bottom line is communication. Deans and chairs must be together both in spirit and in fact. They have to want to support each other and be willing to problem solve to find the best middle ground if there are minor disagreements.

Ultimately, chairs must recognize where the power lies and that there will be times that negotiation and compromise may not work. There are situations in which past precedents come into play, and the dean may have to make a decision based on history for the sake of consistency. While these may be infrequent, they are likely to occur and it is important to the dean and her credibility to be consistent in how people are handled.

The amount of communication with a new dean or department chair will necessarily be greater when the relationship begins. Since many decisions are being dealt with for the first time, it is important for both parties to know that they can get reasonable access to each other if needed. A system needs to be developed to provide for discussion when necessary. Sensitive matters should never be shared in writing through email, messages, or other electronic means that could be hacked, inadvertently sent to the wrong party, or potentially be brought out in a lawsuit. And yes, this does happen.

Some deans and chairs have shared with us that they often speak from car phones while driving home from work. Some schedule fifteen-minute update meetings during the day or share a weekly lunch or a coffee break. What works depends on the individuals and their schedules.

Likewise, you need assurance from the dean that you will have her support for decisions, and there will be many instances when you do not have the chance to first communicate with her. If you and your dean have the advantage of having worked together in the past, and you have a history, you have a huge advantage since you are familiar with each other's styles.

Hopefully, a trust already exists and does not have to be developed from scratch. Trust is crucial, and not immediately given. It must be earned, and that only happens over time and with consistency after dealing with conflicts in the trenches. When a dean has to bring in an outsider, she takes a commensurate risk. While background checks and interviews provide insights into candidates, nothing can replace first-hand, personal experience.

Finally, people take chair positions for different reasons. In the setting described here, you are a tenured professor whose only motivation is to support his school and department. You have no aspirations to move into administration. In this situation, where a difficult and challenging job exists and unpopular decisions will have to be made, you have an advantage since you are aware of the repercussions that are likely to exist but strong enough to weather them. Concerns about your "next job" are not foremost on your mind.

The flip side is that you will have to make unpopular decisions involving people who will be your colleagues after you leave the chair position. Many of these people will never be able to get past their opinion that you failed to support them or their views or actions and will be resentful toward you. Knowing this, you need to decide if your beliefs and principles outweigh the likely price you may have to pay later.

In this particular case, the dean needs to know, from you, that it is okay to remove you from the chair position at any time. This is not your dream job. You are not looking to go anywhere else in the profession. You love being a professor and have no other plans in terms of your career ladder.

The three tenets that you have laid out of students first, civility, and program building are something that you take seriously. Your plan is to be consistent and fair. You have been around long enough to know that as soon as a chair or administrator makes an exception for one person, their credibility is lost and can never be completely recouped. Because of this, the dean needs to know that you cannot function if you believe you are being true to these principles and then your decisions are reversed.

This does not mean that you expect complete carte blanche. Certainly, times will come that you may disagree with her and a decision will not go your way. So you also let her know that you think it is critically important for faculty and staff to observe the two of you working in a supportive manner in which you are consistent in your decision making.

If a dean and chair are working in a positive, effective relationship they will periodically hear a comment to the effect of: "You two always agree with each other." The best thing to do in such a situation is . . . nothing. Keep your mouth shut and think silently to yourself, "Thank goodness."

Line administrators, people who have others reporting to them, make hundreds of decisions daily, and no one makes the best decision every time. However, in your world there is no group in the university that is more important than the students. Secondly, civility is always proper. People should never attack others, period. Disagree or argue respectfully, certainly. But not attack. And finally, while we may be in education, we are also a business. We either provide excellent, high-demand programs that are competitive, build a good name for ourselves, and draw clientele, or we go out of business.

Learnings

1. A clear understanding of the operating principles you believe in as a leader should be made public. It is incumbent on you to plan, budget, teach, and behave on a daily basis in a manner aligned with these principles.
2. Regular communication with faculty and staff related to goals and expectations should be provided both TO them and FROM them.
3. Only take a leadership position when you are fully confident that you and your supervisor share similar values and beliefs.
4. Know what you believe in. Be prepared to publicly state it. Be ready to pay a price for your beliefs . . . but take consolation that if you are true to them, the price is well worth it.

Reflections

1. Two leaders who are either perceived to or are actually in sync can be an intimidating reality to those who thrive on dissension and regularly engage in "splitting behavior." However, it is for this very reason that synchronized leadership can prove one of the key ingredients for success in this scenario.
2. Predictability, especially as manifested between the dean and the chair in this instance, is an associated benefit of synchronized leadership. The structure that it provides will result in a more predictable environment in which individuals can count on certain responses from leaders that become internalized. If successful, this synchronized leadership team can result in the development of a joint super-ego to guide personal decision making by the faculty.
3. As institutional leadership becomes predictable, others in the organization become more comfortable in taking leadership. It is always more effective for individuals to be self-determined as opposed to always having to check in with those in roles of authority.

FOUR

Leadership in Universities

Oxymoron in Action

"If you don't know where you are going, any road will get you there."
—Lewis Carroll's *Alice in Wonderland*

This chapter discusses some of the differences in how leaders are identified, trained, and appointed in different types of institutions—specifically, corporate, pre-K–12 public education, and higher education. It also looks at the inadequacies in one of the most vital procedures conducted by education leaders, the hiring of new faculty, and makes suggestions to address these concerns.

As you begin to consider the Entry Plan and your roles, responsibilities, and background, it occurs to you that leadership at a nonprofit university develops very differently from the leadership in corporate organizations, for-profit educational institutions, or even pre-K–12 schools. While you know you are blessed with a great job as a university professor, you cannot help but take notice when you read an article about leaders in corporate positions making hundreds of thousands of dollars per year and more in their positions. Salaries, stock options, and other perks are definitely eye-catching.

At the same time, you appreciate the fact that you have chosen a profession that allows you an incredible amount of freedom to explore interests that are important to you. And while you will not be attending an annual conference on a Caribbean island or be picked up in the morning by a chauffeur, you know that you have a pretty great life.

You also know from talking with friends in the corporate world, as well as public school colleagues and former students, that there is much you can learn and apply from these other venues to the challenges you are now facing. An overarching theme of many of the conversations that

23

you have had with some of these individuals has centered on having a good grasp on the background of people that you hire and bring into your organization. You have heard, repeatedly, about the importance of careful screening and selection and have decided that it is worth taking a little bit of time to gain a better understanding of training and hiring procedures.

LEADERSHIP PATHS IN CORPORATE ORGANIZATIONS

Leadership paths in for-profit institutions of higher education and not-for-profit institutions of higher education have always been bifurcated. For-profit organizations have a major focus on making money for the employees and stockholders (when they exist).

Competition in open-market economies calls for decisions that consider a number of factors that are not primary concerns in not-for-profit institutions; for instance, locating the most effective low-cost labor available, understanding how to best meet the requirements of tax codes with the least detriment to the organization's profits, and developing and marketing new ideas and products that will continue to draw interest from the buying public, to name a few.

Leadership roles in for-profit institutions, particularly larger Fortune 500 companies, are typically manned (yes, the word "manned" is purposely used) by CEOs with degrees in business. These individuals typically have come up through various positions in business, are often paid phenomenal amounts of money and perks, and report to a board. The boards are often made up of individuals whom the CEOs personally know and recommend for appointments.

Interaction with the buying public is negligible. Layer upon layer of people exist between CEOs and the public . . . and a number of lieutenants make up these layers and are charged with taking care of everyday issues, including dealing with customers and the general public. Major decisions are made behind closed doors, and consumer input in many of these organizations is rarely asked for or considered.

LEADERSHIP PATHS IN PRE-K–12 EDUCATION

Leadership in public education varies greatly from leadership in for-profit education. However, even within education, pre-K–12 school leaders have totally different career paths from college and university leaders. Public education administrators are typically required to hold degrees in a discipline, have actual classroom experience, and hold advanced degrees and training in school leadership.

The normal career ladder usually involves an initial position as an assistant principal or small-school principal. Depending on the location, an individual's progression to larger schools or positions of greater responsibility typically occurs after two to five years. This is a ladder that most public school administrators climb and that often leads to a final leadership position as a senior building or central office administrator.

While no one would argue that money is an important factor to everyone, pre-K–12 public school administrators deal with a much more critical product every day: the children of taxpayers. The vast majority of school districts that vote on budgets pass them annually because they are willing to pay for good education provided in safe, secure schools.

If a private business flubs the design of a widget, it is likely that they will hear very little about it, or at worst receive a phone call or letter of complaint. If a parent thinks their child was unfairly disciplined, a fight occurs, a teacher is arrested, or the state achievement test scores in math are significantly below standards for two or three years in a row, the potential for parents to show up en masse at a board meeting screaming and shouting is not uncommon.

LEADERSHIP PATHS IN HIGHER EDUCATION

Your experiences in higher education differ greatly from your colleagues in the corporate and pre-K–12 public education worlds. Typically, appointments to entry-level positions in higher education administration are often at a department level. Members of the faculty nominate and vote for or against a peer's promotion to department chair.

Appointments are usually for a few years, and reappointments are based on a process that includes several important components: a positive vote of the department, and approval of the department personnel committee, dean, provost, and president. The common reasons for taking such jobs include an interest in a career in leadership, a cultural norm that department members will all "take a turn" at the job, a chance to boost salary for retirement purposes, or a request from peers to take on the role because a need exists and someone has to do it.

In your own case, you had taken the position years before because you thought you might want to pursue a career in administration. However, you missed getting chalk dust on your pants as well as the flexibility that the professoriate provided. And while the chalk dust has been replaced by the glare of a white board, you haven't regretted the decision to return to teaching. And now, because of the problems that exist, the request by peers whom you respect, and the dean's reaching out to you, you have returned for a different reason, and you hope to be able to get the department and its members functioning in a responsive, collegial manner.

In typical circumstances, department chairs are charged with making decisions affecting the same people who ultimately appoint or reappoint

them to—or in some cases, dismiss them from—their positions. So someone in a chair position who really wants to stay in that job, puts his
chances of positive approval in jeopardy any time he makes a decision
that will not be popular with one individual or another. As a result, there
can be strong pressure to compromise one's beliefs in order to keep the
position.

While jobs in the dean's or central offices will narrow the field of
applicants, motivations for these positions may include upward mobility,
an interest in the kind of work being offered, financial reward, or all of
the above.

Regardless of how a person gets into a position, daily problems and
challenges go with the job and need to be remedied. Whether a chair is
appointed from outside of the school, or promotion is given to an insider,
this decision is based on the particular situation or applicant pool. Some
departments may be too small to use an existing faculty member. Or the
fragmentation within the department may be such that no one on the
inside could possibly take the position and be successful.

When this latter situation happens, a faculty member from another
department within the larger college or university might be appointed, or
a retired person with leadership ability might be asked to step in.

HIRING IN HIGHER EDUCATION

The obvious difference between leadership in corporate organizations,
and even pre-K–12 public schools, and higher education is the requirements and training of those who are appointed to positions. MBAs with
job experience are commonly found in the private sector. Advanced degrees and administrative credentials are typically required for individuals in positions in school leadership at the pre-K–12 level.

Higher education is different. Candidates are often solicited, and applicants are asked to provide resumes and references. References are provided through letters from people who know and have worked with the
applicant. Contact information may be requested along with references,
for follow-up by the appointing person or group.

Those involved in screening of applicants in higher education are often restricted in whom they may or may not contact for references. Applicants often provide letters of reference in their application packets. Thus,
they see them beforehand. And even if they do not mail the letters in
themselves (unless letters are specifically earmarked as confidential), it
can be assumed that the applicants have in fact seen these reference letters. Having been on dozens of hiring committees for new faculty and
administrators over the years, you have quite literally read hundreds of
letters of recommendation. Ironically, you have never seen a negative

letter of reference for a candidate who had access to his letters beforehand.

It is a common understanding that no one applying for a position is going to allow a negative letter into their application packet, especially if they know that the letter is critical of them. So this raises a legitimate question: Why bother?

Likewise, if only people identified by the candidate are contacted for references, the same result is likely to occur. Glowing recommendations with a lot of fluff provide little insight into a candidate's actual strengths, weaknesses, and areas for growth. An applicant is not likely to ask someone to be a reference if that person is not going to be supportive. When a candidate has complete control over who is writing or speaking about them, the information gained from these sources is of minimal value since there is no way to measure the objectivity of the sources.

What you have witnessed in your own experiences on hiring committees is that most colleges and universities are so obsessed with what they perceive as fairness, and avoiding potential lawsuits, that they often fail to take advantage of the most important part of the hiring process: comprehensive screening of an applicant's work history. Typically, someone on a hiring committee will have previously worked at an institution that an applicant comes from. Or someone on the committee may have a friend that works at that institution.

However, human resources personnel have told you that you are not allowed to speak to anyone unless that person wrote a letter of recommendation or is listed as a reference. As a result, you have seen numerous cases, some within your own department, of individuals who came across one way in the application process and then were completely different once they were hired.

Some people are professional applicants. They are glib in their letters and interviews, have great body language and patented responses, and know how to present themselves. Unfortunately, authentic performance is not measured in any of these areas. What you think you are going to get based on a candidate's application materials and interview may be quite different from what you see on the job when someone is expected to perform day in and day out. The single best predictor of what a person will do in a new work situation is based on what they have done in a similar situation in the past. Look at what people did previously, and you will have a barometer of their value system.

Competent people involved in hiring pre-K–12 leaders typically work their professional networks to get the best and most comprehensive reviews of candidates. Unions (both teacher and administrator) often check on candidates in sister unions at the site where applicants presently work. Search consultants or personnel directors often talk with people at the location where applicants are presently employed, as well as in districts where they used to work. Board members are often called. Once final candidates have been identified, it is common to have a team of people from a hiring district go and spend a day where the candidate is presently employed and meet with personnel at that location.

At the university level, the process is often much different. Highly competent teaching is important and rewarded in some institutions. In others, research is given a priority. Schools that focus on research and publication often put less emphasis on instructional skills and more on grants, articles, books, and presentations. Thus, someone who is prolific in making contributions to his or her field of study may be seen as a better candidate to take a leadership position than someone who is a strong classroom instructor that receives high evaluations from his or her students.

Neither one of these should be considered the right or proper priority. Research I institutions gain their reputations based on their output. That's who they are. Likewise, schools that take pride in graduates going into various occupation-related fields such as education, certain areas of health care, and law, to name a few, may have a different emphasis.

The approach to awarding leadership positions only gets more pronounced the higher up the ladder one goes in higher education. Some schools are adamant that a vice president or president should hold a PhD (Doctor of Philosophy) degree, rather than an EdD (Doctor of Education), or in some cases, a JD (juris doctorate). The former is oriented toward research and the latter toward pursuing careers in leadership and pedagogy or the practice of law.

Ironically, while the EdD is often more focused on leadership, many in higher education have the idea that a PhD is somehow better suited for such positions. Often, it is other PhDs who hold this belief. In addition, and often because of difficult situations that may have occurred recently at their schools, some boards have felt that individuals with legal experience would be a best choice.

In reality, you know from your own experience that past performance in a similar position is the best indicator of how successful someone is likely to be in a new job. More than what they say in interviews, more than what they present in letters and resumes, performance is the strongest indicator of success. However, higher education institutions almost completely ignore it in many instances.

IMPROVING THE SYSTEM

There is no legal reason in most states to restrict who can or cannot be contacted to give a reference on a candidate. However, when asking people in higher education personnel departments why people other than those provided by the candidate cannot be contacted, the common answer we hear is, "Because that's the way we've always done it." This is an interesting response from an institution that extols the importance of keeping up with the most current practices and is looked upon to shape change and improvement.

Ultimately, leadership is a critical factor in the operation of a highly successful educational organization. When you look at schools, both pre-K–12 and those in higher education, that have highly rated reputations, they invariably have had strong and respected leadership along the way. Rarely have you witnessed schools at any level that have had consistently weak leadership and received high rankings from outside agencies.

Many higher education HR departments focus on what hiring committees cannot do rather than what they should do. Undoubtedly, it is important to treat people fairly and equitably. Primers that include questions that can and cannot be asked are important. Reviewing criteria for job announcements and training individuals who are going to participate in hiring committees are equally critical.

However, these practices are strictly defensive in nature—they are measures that will help prevent potential lawsuits or claims of discrimination. And while this is important, being proactive and thorough is also invaluable. Unless hiring committees can gain an accurate picture of a candidate's past behaviors, what they ultimately get is often little more than a gamble.

These same HR departments could be immeasurably more helpful if they taught committee members how to go about contacting initial references and then using them as springboards to other references that were not provided directly by the candidate. These could be department members, chairs, union representatives, and administrators from candidates' institutions.

Committee members could be trained in how to ask job-related questions that are performance discriminating. They could also be taught how to "listen." In other words, they may get negative responses on a candidate: "He was too progressive, we are a traditional institution and he didn't fit." This kind of response might beg further questions because in some cases this might be exactly what the hiring institution needs. Also, the totality of recommendations should be considered, not just a response from one individual.

Applications could be improved upon by asking for confidential letters of reference. Ironically, many universities use head-hunting firms for hiring people into administrative positions. Interestingly, these newly hired administrators often come to a position and stay for three to five years and then leave to move up the ladder. However, the same approaches are not used by most universities to hire professors, many of whom stay in their jobs for twenty to thirty years.

Certainly, the academic credentials of new employees in higher education are an important consideration that needs to be taken into account when hiring occurs. However, as one of the most important actions that you will perform, hiring decisions need to consider a number of factors: academic and experiential background, potential to contribute, interests of the candidate that would fit with the environment of your institution, communication skills, interpersonal skills, and other relevant concerns. But on top of all of these, and most important, a clear record of successful past performance is critical.

Learnings

1. The practice of having faculty determine their leader, and then expecting that leader to make difficult decisions that may not be popular with some of those same faculty members, is a contradiction.
2. Colleges and universities often do poor jobs of screening candidates for leadership positions.
3. Higher education leaders typically have little academic or experiential background in leadership prior to going into their positions. As a result, they need extra support, training, and mentoring in learning how to operate in their roles.

Reflections

1. Do not underestimate the "ambivalence to authority" that all university-related personnel possess . . . it is the one common characteristic of all of those involved in the daily work of the academy. Despite the inherent conflicts, the system is successful in numbers of situations, while failing miserably in others (and many levels in between).
2. Quality of personnel is one of the most important factors in determining the reputation of a university. It is important for leaders to lead . . . and part of that charge should be looking at procedures being used to identify and develop future leaders. Activities that work should be supported; procedures that are not sound should be examined and replaced.
3. It will be necessary from time to time to encourage others in the chain of command to back up decisions. This support should always be fair and justified, although not always necessarily equitable (especially if student welfare and/or program integrity might be at risk).

FIVE
Leadership in Departments

"Trust is built with consistency."

—Lincoln Chafee

Trust has a number of different meanings. When used as a noun, the dictionary uses descriptors like *conviction, belief, reliability,* and *consistency.* Perhaps the most important elements of trust in the realm of school leadership involve the need for transparency and predictability. This does not mean that everyone believes in you and likes you personally. However, they do know what you stand for and regularly observe you behaving in ways that are consistent with those beliefs.

Not only is it important for you to be consistent, you must hold every faculty member up to the same standards of behavior and performance and respond in kind. Regardless of who the faculty might be, rewards and sanctions need to be predictable and fair across the board in order to gain trust.

At the same time, you need to understand that when you say "no" to someone, it may result in resentment, dislike, and even vindictiveness. If asked if they "trust" you, some individuals will answer with a resounding "NO!" To them, trust and respect are defined as someone who is in accord with their needs and interests, not necessarily the needs and interests of the students and institution.

When put in this framework, leaders might want to focus on principled predictability as a goal that will develop higher degrees of trust. In other words, a principled leader is one who will do the right thing for the right reasons regardless of the feelings of those who may be disadvantaged by particular decisions.

With time and experience, you have learned that effectiveness over the long haul, and by this we mean several years under different regimes, is not based on meeting everyone's needs. If every individual in a rela-

31

tively large institution loves you, the chances are pretty good that you have not made difficult decisions that were consistently in the best interests of the organization. As Arthur Bloch once said, "Friends come and go but enemies accumulate." This is undoubtedly true and certainly applies to those in leadership roles, but strong leaders with strong positive values can survive this.

STRESSES OF LEADERSHIP

Leadership is hard. It can be lonely. It often means loss of sleep and isolation from immediate faculty that you are usually in contact with each day. It may mean accepting a cold shoulder in a hallway, having noisy conversations with union representatives, and learning to handle self-doubt.

Effective leaders will have people responding to them across a wide spectrum. At one end are those who will agree with virtually everything they say and do in order to stay in their good graces. People who do this may simply be insecure and react to others in this way throughout their lives. In other cases, some may feel vulnerable or fearful.

There are those who operate between the extremes who feel personally and professionally secure. They are not looking to gain anything by giving a compliment or sharing a concern.

At the other end are those who carry resentment toward a specific person in leadership or toward authority in general. Regardless of what a leader proposes, they will find fault with it and make it as difficult as possible for the leader to implement any initiatives.

Ultimately, a leader needs to be able to identify what he is hearing at a given time. While the three categories outlined above are fairly broad, the fact is that people may shift from one to another depending on the situation. Leadership is situational. Regardless of what is occurring, an effective leader needs to have a good radar and be able to listen, sort, and choose the information being given that is most valuable.

We have all witnessed new leaders who nod their heads in agreement with everyone who approaches them. They want to be liked and accepted. In one case a leader found himself in a bind when he learned that a commitment to one person to teach a particular class required disappointing another person that had also been promised a section of the same course to teach. The new chair quickly learned to use the word "tentative" with all faculty when discussing course assignments. However, he also paid a price when the faculty member who was "bumped" was unsympathetic and made disparaging remarks about him.

As a leader you must find and develop support systems. You need to identify individuals you respect that will tell you what you need to hear. These may not always be the messages that you want to hear. Without this, there is a tendency to "believe your own press." People in your department may feel uncomfortable about giving you critical and constructive feedback, and as a result. you may have a tendency to convince yourself you must be doing everything right.

In addition to being uncomfortable about telling you that you messed up, some faculty may be fearful that doing so could have repercussions. And of course, there are also the faculty that just plain love the drama attached to walking the hallways and sharing conversations in whispers about you and how your brain apparently turned to mush when you got this job, because you are suddenly making nothing but dumb decisions and you "just don't get it" anymore.

Everyone, including department chairs, wants to be liked and appreciated. The chances of being liked and appreciated by everyone in your department, college, or university are slim to none. This is not a position for the weak of heart. Anyone taking on a job of this sort must have a clear and realistic understanding of who they are, what they stand for, how they conduct themselves, and how much affirmation they actually need.

You think back to your original appointment as a department chair and an occasion when you called the vice president's office to ask for information and were told you would get it the next day. You waited a day, and then another, and called again. You were told once more that it would be forthcoming. After three days, the information still was not received.

Then you called the vice president directly and told her what happened. She went to the person who should have sent the information out and let him know about your call. You got the information immediately. However, you also heard from your assistant that the person who sent it from the VP's office was at lunch that day in the canteen and was sharing "what a difficult pain in the ass" you were.

HELPING ENSURE SUCCESS

To succeed in this job, you are well aware that you need to identify people of integrity on the faculty and staff and make a point of listening to them, seeking their advice, and learning from them. Likewise, out of fairness, you know that it is important to provide the same ear to all staff. You are aware that if unproductive individuals clearly do not support you and are slandering and sabotaging you, this is not necessarily a bad thing. The idiom, "You can judge a person by his friends," has some truth to it. Likewise, you can judge a person by his enemies. However, when such behaviors become public, they must be contained (more on this later).

In addition to taking advice, the dean suggests a strategy she has seen used by other chairs in the college. They ask faculty and staff to provide feedback anonymously. Since a lot of people are sensitive about sharing anything electronically, such as through email or surveys, she suggests you put a note in each faculty member's mailbox once or twice a year. It might simply say that you are looking to improve your skills as a chair and you would appreciate their thoughts.

Potential respondents would be asked to share the two or three things that they think you are doing right and the two or three things they think you could do better. They should also be asked to be as specific as possible and to give any recommendations they might have. Their comments can be placed in a blank envelope and given to the department secretary or to a member of the dean's office staff. Everyone would be assured that all comments will be read by you alone.

Depending on the faculty, you may or may not receive much response to this. However, if you do get constructive suggestions, they can in fact be a source for growth and improvement. If you do not get much response, you know that you have at least modeled a willingness to be open and listen to others, whether they decide to take advantage of the opportunity or not. Some leaders who have used this approach have even made the comments public along with their responses. Taking constructive criticism and acting on it is a great way to build credibility with faculty and staff.

LEADERSHIP TURNED UPSIDE DOWN

Just as the path to leadership in higher education is different depending upon whether it is through the private or public route, the conduct of leaders is also very different. Certainly, there are legal parameters that must be observed in all organizations. However, some might say that higher education looks like the private sector turned upside down. In the private sector, the chief executive officer and president hold a great deal of power.

Depending on who is in these positions, the amount of advice provided by subordinates will vary. Some CEOs are autocratic and will make decisions with little input. These leaders expect those under them to be compliant and follow the directives they have been given. This expectation repeats itself as initiatives are implemented down the chain of command.

Higher education, in its best and most productive form, takes direction from its faculty. This does not mean that faculty members take turns walking through the president's office to review the questions and concerns of the day in order to advise the president on what she should do. However, faculty governance, effectively run, has major, broad-based decision-making power in matters such as the institution's "brand," personnel hiring, retention, tenure, and firing. Likewise, faculty cooperation, and sometimes consent, is required along with administrative approval in determining programs and initiatives.

At the department level where you work, faculty is typically responsible for organizing programs within departments, developing schedules and assignments, outlining procedures for dealing with student programs and activities, and establishing protocols for handling department affairs. And most importantly, at the department level, the faculty identifies and appoints the same leader who is being charged with their supervision.

This organizational pattern, which operates in many universities and colleges and is supported by strong unions, makes governance interesting. Faculty, backed up by union membership, is the most educated and sophisticated workforce in the world. So on the one hand, faculty has a great deal of responsibility and authority for how the institution is administered; on the other hand, they are the recipients of those decisions. With such a vested interest, it would seem impossible to operate in an objective, well-intentioned manner. However, most do just that.

Having observed thousands of higher education faculty in multiple institutions, one can only marvel at the ability of most faculties to do the right things for the right reasons. The vast majority are talented people who have been willing to take positions that often provide far less in pay and recognition and potential advancement than would be available to individuals employed in the private sector. With little pressure placed on them from external sources, most put in countless hours and spend money out of their own pockets to keep up with their professions by attending conferences, and purchasing books and online resources, technology, and travel. The vast majority willingly volunteer to sit on committees, attend events, and spend hundreds of hours reviewing student work, as well as advising their students.

There is a certain understanding professors share as respected members of the academy. This transcends the pay, recognition, and any reinforcement provided by other external systems. It is the respect of other colleagues and staff. It is not often talked about publicly or even acknowledged, but those who walk the hallowed halls know exactly what it is. Some get it. Some don't. It isn't given. It can only be earned.

Because of this odd, almost nonsensical manner of operating, leaders in higher education find that much of their ability to function is a result of their power of persuasion. While certain legislated power goes along with positions, it is extremely rare to see tenured professors dismissed. For most, tenure provides a lifetime contract. And at the department level, with the faculty being the determining body deciding who gets and keeps the chair job, it is incumbent on the chair to regularly talk with faculty to get a sense of their perspectives and try to work with them in a collegial, persuasive manner in order to get things done.

Regardless of how much merit an initiative may have, people do not like taking orders or being mandated to do things in a certain way. Consequently, in an environment where faculty already have a great deal of individual as well as collective power, the only real way to get them to buy into a change is through the ability of chairs and deans to show them the benefits of any initiative and to convince them that it is ultimately in the best interests of the students and faculty.

Learnings

1. Transparency and predictability are critically important characteristics that a chair can provide.
2. Leaders need to be absolutely certain before making promises. It is okay to tell a person you cannot make a commitment at this time. It is also important to let them know when you do make a commitment, and to get back to them in a timely manner with a response.
3. "No" is not a four-letter word.
4. Asking people to give feedback on your leadership ability can be enlightening and helpful. It can also show people that you are willing to make yourself vulnerable.

Reflections

1. One of the toughest—if not the toughest job in the academy is that of department chair. The role comes with all of the responsibility but not with a lot of authority. Chairs have to walk a delicate line of supporting colleagues but also moving department-related business forward.
2. Collegial relationships with a few members of the department may continue until the time the chair has to say "no" to a faculty request. This has to be handled with care and respect; otherwise, bad feelings can quickly evolve into active campaigning to remove a chair as the leader of the department.
3. With the day-to-day challenges of leading a department, it is often a good exercise for a chair to work with faculty to identify several goals that they can work on together. In turn, the chair should post these goals in a place that he sees on a daily basis. With all of the mandates and demands that take place each day in a chair's life, this visible list of goals provides a point of focus.
4. The governance of higher education makes no logical sense, yet it works for the most part because of good people.

SIX

Getting Started

"The evil is half cured whose cause we know."

—Shakespeare

Like the vast majority of educators, you are a humanist. Most educators enter the field because they like people and want to make a difference in the lives of those they come in contact with. Conflict does not come easily for anyone, but it is particularly difficult for most educators.

Almost any school that has undergone significant change has typically tried to do it in the least painful manner. This is the humane thing to do and the right thing to do. However, there are times that small steps do not get a department or college or larger university to the ends they need to reach. At the extreme, we have witnessed strikes and boycotts and sit-ins. These are rare, but they are real events that sometimes bring certain harsh realities to administrations and boards.

As a newly appointed chair in a department that has been dysfunctional for an extended period of time, you realize that you no longer have the luxury of taking small steps. You make a commitment to your dean as well as to yourself that you will do the "right things," but you let her know that these right things may well result in fallout. In taking on this job, you know you may lose friendships and there will be periods of isolation. However, you also believe there is a larger cause: providing quality programs to students. In addition, on a personal level, there is a secondary goal: being able to look in the mirror and acknowledging that you have done the right things for the right reasons.

With this in mind, you decide to take an approach that a friend once described as "percolating." As he described it, it is a matter of trying to affect change through a simultaneous bottom-up and top-down effort. As already established, you do not have time on your side; consequently, you need to continue to work with faculty to take small progressive steps

37

where possible. At the same time, you need to be willing to be directive in important matters related to students, civility, program building, and other critical concerns that require attention.

OPENING THE DOOR

In getting started, an important first step in outlining expectations includes taking the opportunity to communicate the news about your appointment to the faculty and inviting them to stop in for informal discussions prior to the start of the school year. If done during the summer, when the faculty is not officially "on the clock," many will decline this opportunity, and that is fine. Summer is their time.

However, some will want to take advantage of the chance to meet with you to talk and share and will make an appointment to stop by. This is a chance to discuss things with them in a more relaxed atmosphere without the hustle and bustle that typically occurs during the school year when faculty, staff, and students are on campus.

Meeting during the vacation period allows you to talk about personal matters related to health and family and how their vacation time is going, as well as professional matters, to see if there is anything you can do for them in preparation for the school year. It is also a chance to introduce the three tenets (commitment to students, civility, and building excellent programs) that you plan to focus on. It is a chance to talk a little bit about what the tenets mean to you and ask them for any suggestions they might have to put them into practice.

People appreciate the opportunity to talk to the boss. And if you want to build your credibility, one of the best ways to do it is to listen carefully and act on any suggestions that are given to you. A follow-up note to anyone who has provided an idea that has resulted in an action is a great way to further develop a relationship.

While these meetings are an opportunity to spread your message, the three beliefs must be acted on each day through your conduct. Placing these beliefs on an attractive poster board in your office or the room used for faculty meetings, stating them in conversations with faculty, and publicly referring to them in decision making, will help to illustrate their importance and value to the ongoing business of the department.

Departments regularly deal with high-priority decisions, such as: Should we run an online program? Should we offer Saturday classes? Should we block-schedule classes rather than offer them once a week over the course of a semester? One way to give consideration to faculty and students on questions like this that effect their lives is to simply ask them. Seeking out opinions can be done through discussions in classes or with an online survey using one of the free or inexpensive programs that are available to the public.

A number of other examples can be made here, as well. Of particular priority, due to the sensitive nature of the subject, is dealing with faculty or student personnel matters. Invariably, students will periodically complain about how they were treated by a professor. Most of those issues are relatively straightforward, such as whether a grade should be the A that the student believes she deserves or the C that the professor gave her.

However, there are also times when complaints are potentially more sensitive. This might include the student who believes he was discriminated against or was the victim of sexual harassment. If our second tenet is to behave in a civil manner with all those with whom we come in contact, and we talk and plan on how we will conduct ourselves in relation to that tenet, then commitment to following it should help prevent such incidents from occurring in the first place. Openly discussing what it means, sharing suits that have occurred, and providing staff development on the topic are all useful means for doing this.

You can recall one year when the dean asked an attorney who was an education specialist to present a speech to faculty and staff entitled: "When you can be held personally responsible." Participation was voluntary, yet it was one of the most highly subscribed events of the semester.

Getting belief statements out to the public as soon as possible is important. Since not everyone is around during the summer, the "Welcome Back to School Day" that typically takes place just prior to classes beginning is a chance to share your thoughts on the beliefs and how you see the department operating with the start of the new year.

Even if several people have stopped by and had one-on-one conversations with you, reviewing the tenets often is a wise move. Saying them and making them public is important. The only thing that is more important is what follows . . . acting on them.

COMMUNICATION

Most people leave that first day faculty meeting feeling positive and optimistic about having a good year. Professors and staff have returned from well-deserved vacations, people are happy to reunite with colleagues, and energy levels are high. While this is the norm in the vast majority of higher education departments, things are different in yours. Because of the history of the last few years, the entire department cannot be in one room together. As a result, you are restricted in getting your message out and have had to do it through individual meetings with those people that have come into the office.

In addition, while the three operating principles are the message you want to get across, you also see the importance of doing business differently. One strategy you have decided upon is a regular department "newsletter." Modern equivalents of newsletters (e.g., e-news, etc.) have made communication easy to create and distribute—both in a real and in a virtual environment.

A newsletter is a simple but tangible vehicle for sharing information with the department. It provides you with a means to get information out quickly through electronic means. It is a chance to recognize accomplishments as well as share information of interest. While not as powerful as the two-way communication that occurs in faculty meetings, it at least provides a vehicle to let people know about important information that affects the department. And, just as importantly, it also provides you with assurance that everyone is hearing the same message at the same time.

Within the splinter groups in the department, some faculty members believe that requests by certain individuals have been given consideration over others. Charges have been made that various chairs in the past have shown favoritism when giving out choices of courses to teach, assigning rooms, or directing financial resources to some members over others. You realize that this is a trap you need to avoid and that the best way to achieve this is through transparency. The newsletter is one key instrument in your toolkit that will help you reach this goal.

While the newsletter is useful for the reasons listed above, it serves an even more important purpose: It is one example of how the department is actually conducting business in a different manner. The provost made it clear that this is the last chance for this group to come together, to heal, and to work cohesively. All of the attempts made thus far have failed. Some members of the department do not think his threat is authentic. They see the department as too big and important to be dissolved.

However, you do believe him. You know that there are other ways of delivering programs and that he is serious. Consequently, you have decided that changes must be made that are visible and real.

In addition to its function as a way of communicating, along with being a symbol of how business is being done differently, you realize that this period of time as a chair will be much different than what you experienced in the past. Back in the good old days when the department was "normal," you did not have to feel guarded about everything you said or did. Not so in the present. You realize the need to treat people as fairly as possible and as openly as possible. You also know that your definition of fairness will differ from the definition of a faculty member who does not like a decision that you made.

IN A DYSFUNCTIONAL DEPARTMENT, THIS CAN BE A LONELY JOB

You have also seen new chairs that were worried about their own reappointments. As a result, many of them would continuously try to make everyone happy all of the time. This never works, because ultimately decisions meet reality and someone is not going to be satisfied. Two people cannot occupy the same preferred classroom. Two people cannot teach the same course. If promises are made and broken, your reputation is going to be damaged beyond repair. As a mentor once told you, "Once you break a trust, you can never get it back. Better to be damned for saying *no* once than *yes* twice."

You have read a number of articles in recent years about the importance of building trusting relationships. Several authors have talked about the need for leaders to be able to "draw out" from an emotional bank account when they have to make difficult decisions. This concept makes a great deal of sense. When you consider situations that you have been involved in with close family and friends, you know there have been times that someone did something or said something that you did not approve of.

However, because you had a strong emotional tie to that person, you forgave them and moved on. If the same thing happened with a stranger or colleague that you did not know well, you might decide to ignore or distance yourself from that person permanently. You have no need to give them loyalty, you do not share any history with them, you do not live with them, and as a result, there is no emotional tie that binds you.

Some faculty and staff will observe what you do when faced with a decision they might not like or agree with. But if they respect you and feel that they have a relationship with you, this gives you some capital to draw on when you have to make a decision that they might not like. Hopefully, they will try to see your point of view and still stand by you even though they are not happy in that moment.

As a result, you are aware that the dean has put her faith in you to do the right thing. She understands that you are not going to be able to satisfy all of the people all of the time, but she does expect that you will treat everyone fairly. And while the term "fairly" is subjective, she believes that the two of you, who are most reasonable people, will be able to look at the difficult decisions you will have to make and be satisfied that they are consistent and equitable based on the specific situations, history, and people involved.

YOU, THE DEAN, AND COMMUNICATION

The dean's role in this process cannot be understated. She too realizes that you are going to be around a large group of people each day and that you will often feel isolated and without a lot of immediate support. You know from experience that you absolutely cannot confide in one faculty member about a difficult situation that has occurred involving another faculty member. Doing this (i.e., confiding in one faculty member over another) is the kiss of death. At some point, the person you confide in may be upset and unhappy with you. If this occurs, he could quote some of the things you have said to him about others.

You have also witnessed a faculty member going back to the union representative and sharing comments made by a chair in supposedly private conversations. The rule your mother taught you, to never talk about others behind their backs, was a wise one. And while doing so will help keep you out of trouble, it does little to quell feelings of self-doubt that will occur when you are faced with difficult decisions — especially since you cannot depend on others internal to the department for advice.

This is where the dean comes in. She faces the same kinds of challenges every day and having been a department chair herself, and now a dean for several years, she realizes how important it is that she provides you with a sounding board if you need it. Her reassurance that you can contact her at any time is important. You both know she has a heavy schedule, but she points out that if there is ever an emergency you should not hesitate to have her interrupted. Otherwise, she lets you know she reads emails throughout the day, and if you put a note in the subject line in capitals, she will do her best to make sure she responds as requested.

The dean also suggests the two of you schedule time for coffee every couple of weeks. While you will communicate regularly on issues, this will be a time to just reflect and catch up on how things are going. This provides you a chance to fill in details on events that have occurred, pick each other's brains on what is going on (or might be coming down the road), and have an opportunity for a bit of therapy. Most importantly, it provides a dependable refuge to provide feedback and brainstorm potential solutions to seemingly intractable problems.

The dean also lets you know that there are fellow chairs in the college who are well experienced and supportive. As a long term faculty member, you have worked with several of these people over the years and know whose opinions you trust and respect. You also know which of them you feel comfortable with when sharing confidential matters. The dean tells you that some of the chairs meet for lunch every week or two in order to have private, informal discussions about matters of interest. This forum would be a great opportunity for you to share your own concerns as well as hear about the issues and recommendations of others.

With the newsletter now in place, and feeling some comfort in your relationship with the dean, you are ready to think more about the department and the big picture. As you reflect, you realize there are two important groups that you need to deal with: one is the office staff and the other is the faculty. Within these two groups there are several areas that need to be addressed: personnel, physical plant, operations, and program.

THE OFFICE: PERSONNEL

There is no question in your mind that the teaching faculty is the most important body affecting students. They are the major point of contact for students and ultimately deliver the product that you want to offer—a sound education.

As noted previously, one of the ironies of your department is that you have many people who are effective in their classrooms with students but at the same time are unable to work collegially with their peers. The behavioral standards provided by the state, as well as professional organizations, mandate a level of professionalism by students in order to be awarded credentials. However, many of the same people who are supposed to be educating these students on how to be professional are unable to behave in a professional manner themselves.

Several have refused to be in the same room with colleagues, much less show a willingness to talk through issues in a civil manner. In fact, some are still publicly making remarks that are unprofessional and unethical. This sometimes occurs openly in meetings and at other times occurs through eye rolling, avoiding contact with colleagues, and other unprofessional behaviors.

As you think more deeply about this, you realize that there are no real choices. Either concerns get addressed or the department dissolves. With this in mind, people either have to live by the rules, both in spirit and in fact, or they need to leave. Expectations need to be clear and behaviors consistently monitored. Where possible, changes will have to be made.

Without question, personnel are the most critical group affecting the success of the department. The failure of personnel to work together in a collegial and professional manner attests to this. As department chair, you have two primary groups to deal with in this area: support personnel, including your office staff, and department faculty.

The dean has assured you that you have her confidence in making difficult decisions, and as you take time during the summer to review personnel and departmental functions, you realize that some of your support staff is part of the problem. You have noticed the climate deteriorate in the department office. As you think about the past when people got along well, you realize that faculty and staff regularly walked through the office, stopped and chatted while having a cup of coffee, and shared updates on both their professional and personal lives.

Each fall one of the department faculty would host a party at his home that virtually all faculty and staff would help to organize and attend. Activities included a good share of alcohol, games, jokes, and stories. This does not happen now. Today there is a disconnect, not only within the faculty, but between some of the faculty and staff. Finally, you think about the initial conversation you had with the dean at the beginning of this process: Will you be up to the task of engaging in difficult conversations with staff, and will you remain committed to making the decisions necessary to effect changes if warranted?

You are fully aware that the staff is competent; they do not purposely initiate problems, nor have they consciously facilitated what has occurred in recent years. However, you also realize that some of them have developed strong alliances with certain faculty and former chairs, and this has caused them to be placed in "camps" that include other support staff and often some faculty members.

In doing your homework with the Office of Human Resources, you find that the dean has the authority to move some of these staff into other departments and areas in the college. They will not lose anything in terms of pay or benefits, and in fact a change in assignment would take them out of the line of fire between some of the faculty groups. You know from conversations that they have often felt caught between different members and groups of faculty and they have had to listen to complaints that are really outside of their areas of responsibility.

They have also witnessed some of the nasty interactions that have taken place between faculty members. In addition, the regular turnover of chairs has sometimes placed them in very awkward situations, including reports of staff observing the misuse of funds, equipment, and other resources that are concerning to you. You realize that some of these possible transgressions could be highly sensitive and more complicated down the road.

You also know that you must always talk with the dean before making an important decision. It is absolutely essential that she and the provost support any critical action that you take. In this case, you let them know that you may recommend the removal of some members of the office staff to other positions. You share why, and you assure the dean and the provost that you will meet with each of the office staff individually and explain what you plan to do and why it is in the staff's, as well as the department's, best interest.

Working with the dean, and with the help of the provost and other chairs and deans in the university, you learn of opportunities to move some of these personnel to positions that would be kinder and healthier.

Since moving individuals from their positions is often emotionally charged, it is important that you are fully confident that your decision is in the best interest of the department. It should also be noted that hiring new people to replace those who have been transferred is not a simple process.

It is absolutely critical that extensive background checks and personal interviews take place that assure you that replacement staff will be able to establish an office environment that is friendly and business-like, but free of personal relationships that would hinder your efforts to rebuild the department. Once new staff is hired, regular meetings will be needed to discuss operations and any matters of concern that may arise.

THE OFFICE: PHYSICAL PLANT

One of the best times to make change in any organization is during a period of major transition. Whether the organization is new, or reorganization is taking place, this period provides an opportunity in which people expect changes will occur. Energy levels are high, and there is excitement and expectation. Many people look forward to changes. As a new chair, this provides you a unique opportunity to get some things done with minimal resistance. It is that one time when you do not have to worry about hearing, "But in the past we . . ."

As you sit at your desk in your first days on the job, it strikes you that one way to quickly show your commitment to this transition through visible, physical changes. This should start with the first thing people see when they visit the department—the physical space in the office.

You have already replaced office staff. Having gained support from upper administration, you put in requests to have the walls painted and some of the old, decrepit furniture replaced. In addition, and more importantly, you recognize that visitors sometimes enter the office. If staff is busy, visitors take a seat and might be there several minutes before anyone notices them. The office is set up in a traditional manner, with a counter that provides a barrier between visitors and office personnel. You share your concerns with the new office staff, that people are often not noticed and the physical barrier of the counter does not send the kind of message that all of you are trying to convey.

You ask their thoughts on this and solicit any ideas that they might have to improve the physical environment. Using their suggestions, as well as your own ideas, you let the dean know that you would like the counter removed. And . . . you want this done within the week. You remind her that you agreed that change needs to occur and it needs to occur quickly.

In place of the counter, desks are physically situated so that visitors and staff will make eye contact as soon as someone enters the office. A brighter environment is one step forward. This is one of the easy yet significant actions that will help you move forward.

THE OFFICE: PROCEDURES

While the previous office staff did a fine job under difficult conditions, you realize that this time of transition gives you an opportunity to address some of the concerns you have had about past office practices. You also want to be sure that the new staff is committed to the changes and practices that you want to initiate in the office.

Another department chair in the college shares with you that she experienced success by developing rubrics with her office staff that addressed various practices. She said that engaging them in this process allowed everyone to share their perceptions of what helps to establish a positive or negative office environment.

Since you think this is a great idea, you let the dean know that you want to spend a day with the staff talking about your shared vision for the office and what they need, as well as what you need, to make that vision a reality. The dean consents and assures you that someone from her office will cover calls and visitors to your department so that your personnel can spend time on this task.

Once the day arrives, and following a breakfast together, you ask the staff to share their impressions of offices that they have visited that left a positive impression on them, and why. This includes educational as well as medical, business, and other offices that they have visited. Using the descriptors they share, you jointly develop a statement of a "model office."

Next, you ask your staff to list the common practices that they regularly engage in. Some of these include answering the telephone, responding to requests, welcoming visitors, completing paperwork, interacting with faculty, engaging in correspondence, and working with personnel from other offices in the university.

Together, you develop a rubric for each item and identify four points on a scale:

1. Describe the practice when it left a bad impression on you.
2. Describe the practice when it left a poor impression on you.
3. Describe the practice when it made a positive impression on you.
4. Describe the practice when it made an extremely positive impression on you.

This exercise provides you with an opportunity to cooperatively develop a set of norms and expectations in a nonthreatening environment. It also allows time for discussion and examples. For instance, you might share how you went to dinner over the weekend and waited a half hour for your food and the waiter never came by to let you know what was going on. This leads to the question: Do people sometimes visit our office and feel ignored?

Someone else might share their recent experience sitting in a doctor's office for over two hours waiting to be seen because the doctor double and triple books patients as a normal procedure. These are the kinds of practices that leave terrible impressions . . . and yet how often do we seek out those we serve to determine how they, in turn, view us?

This activity provides a chance to learn from one another and at the same time develop ideas for positive practices that you want to become norms in the department office. Finally, as a chair, it gives you a useful tool to use when discussing practices and personnel behaviors in the future. This may be during an evaluation process or when you want to give someone a pat on the back, or when you need to redirect an individual's behavior. Since these are to become part of the department's expectations, having staff involved in their construction will also aid in staff developing a vested interest in their implementation.

School leaders often fail to value the importance of their support staff. These people are the first ones that new visitors come in contact with when calling or coming to campus. An administrative assistant can make or break his boss. If yours is unfriendly, or inefficient, or lacking in skills, his failure to perform well reflects on you. Likewise, having people in these positions that know how to greet visitors and respond to faculty and other professionals can be a tremendous asset.

This honeymoon period when you first come on the job is a great opportunity to look at policies and practices and make changes, since you were not involved in developing them. You can "get away" with ideas with a new staff that is open to suggestions much more easily than you can with one that is entrenched and might feel you do not appreciate them if you were to make recommendations for improvement. This is particularly true if the existing staff were the ones that developed the existing standards and may feel they have ownership of them.

In your situation, where not only are you new to the job, but also several of the office staff are new as well, you have a great opportunity to eliminate ineffective practices and try out new ones. Take advantage of new starts. Often, administrative assistants in deans' offices have worked in departments and have positive reputations. Asking the dean's administrative assistant or someone else in her office to coach new office staff can be very helpful to the person in your office that is new to their position.

As a long-term faculty member, you know that there are very few secrets in a college. Everyone is pretty much known to everyone else. Whether deserved or not, reputations are attached to individuals in all positions. You know your office will be seen as a "good office to deal with," or not. There typically is not much middle ground. Bringing in new office staff, reconstructing, retooling, and sending a message that all members of your department are committed by their words and actions to treating others with respect, modeling civility at all times, and building a positive program will assist in building the kind of reputation you strive to develop.

MONITORING THE CHANGES

As a professor, one of the things that you have learned about organizations is that rhetoric can be valuable. However, you also know that there is no guarantee that rhetoric always translates into effectiveness. To truly determine whether your efforts make a difference, you realize that you have to model what you will preach to others: that we all need to be willing to be vulnerable and periodically assess our progress.

This means you will require accurate feedback on how well the changes that you have implemented have actually worked in practice. One of the best ways to accomplish this is to ask people. One informal means of collecting information is through the use of networks. Within virtually every large organization, and certainly within universities, there are individuals and small groups that are highly respected and tuned into what is going on.

Your building's maintenance supervisor is the long-term union representative for civil service staff. She has a reputation as a straight shooter, and you have had a long-term friendly relationship with her. She is one of those people who will tell you what you need to hear, good or bad. Likewise, the dean's administrative assistant regularly meets with the administrative assistants from all of the departments. He hears all of the gossip that goes on and is tuned in to how the different offices are perceived.

It is easy to be consumed by gossip, and you have to be wary of allowing it to consume you. The bulk of whispering that takes place should be ignored. You could spend entire days running it down. At the same time, persistent gossip or emotionally charged gossip may need to be curbed. While the rumors that float through the hallways may not always be accurate, they still have the power to affect perceptions.

In dealing with fellow faculty, you have your own network of colleagues that you have known for a long time and upon whom you can rely for honesty and candor. Regular conversations over lunch as well as parking lot conversations can give you a pretty good idea of how your efforts are perceived. It can even be helpful to ask them periodically what they are hearing about the department and the efforts that are being made.

Finally, and perhaps most importantly, more formal means of gathering views from students also need to occur. Higher education institutions regularly survey pending graduates on their perceptions of their academic programs. This is also a chance to explore their observations of the department in other areas. You should take the opportunity to question them about non-instructional areas such as the receptivity and helpfulness of the office staff, professors, administration, and various university offices that they have used during their time in the program.

FROM OFFICE TO FACULTY

Developing a set of broad plans for dealing with faculty and staff is an important first step for someone coming into a leadership position. The difference between your department today and the department makeup you were used to in the past is the obvious dysfunction that has developed in recent years.

You and the dean have both agreed that you will start the school year with a positive and optimistic approach. However, you have also agreed that if and when problem behaviors arise, you will deal with them immediately, whenever it is reasonable to do so.

In addition to this, you realize from your own observations, as well as your conversations with the dean, that you are not going to be able to alter some of the serious problems that exist through newsletters, pep talks, or mandates. They will require one-on-one intervention and some of the "difficult conversations" that the dean spoke of when you were first appointed.

DEALING WITH DYSFUNCTIONAL PERSONNEL

With this in mind, chapters 7 through 12 describe six different cases. None of these cases are based on one particular individual. Each main character is a composite resulting from a collection of observations, discussions, and experiences. Further, sequences of events and reactions are a composite of some history, some reality, and some fantasy based on what would have, could have, or should have happened according to the author.

Having qualified this fiction, it should be noted that the problems described will not be uncommon to many readers who have spent time in educational organizations—higher education and otherwise. In addition, it should be noted that the conceptual base for approaching the fictional characters described is not a fiction. Looking through the lens of Passive, Passive-Aggressive, and Aggressive personality types as individuals slide back and forth through this spectrum in the cases described in the next chapters is not uncommon. Leaders need a stable frame of reference for dealing with their colleagues, and these categories provide a starting point.

The second component of the framework for the chair and dean is reflecting on the psychological needs of fun (enjoyment), power (this might be the belief that one's work makes a difference, but might also involve one's perception of control over others), and affiliation (belonging, friendship, connection). This concept of needs is widely popular, and many have found it a useful tool in how they view and assess others.

Finally, since we know that broad-stroke approaches rarely are effective in dealing with change, it is important to acknowledge that leaders must deal with issues one at a time, one person at a time. A dean or department chair needs to use the kind of frameworks described above, or whatever they have found that works for them, and adapt them to their immediate situation.

Leaders must have good radar. If they sense a potential problem, they need to try to intervene before it becomes a major problem. This may occur through conversation, simple schedule changes, or some other type of support that can be garnered and provided to an individual. Heading the problem off at the pass helps avoid more complicated problems later on. Unfortunately, not all problems are resolved this easily.

The cases described in the next chapters are more complex, and in some instances had already affected students and other professional personnel and required handling on an individual basis.

Learnings

1. Change requires a clear picture of where you want to be in relation to where you are now.
2. To gain a clear picture of where you are now, ask people.
3. Once you decide on the specific goals you want to achieve, communicate them and make them public. Public goals are more likely to be met than those limited to being shared in-house.
4. Leadership can be lonely. No, leadership *will* be lonely. Be prepared for that and choose those you confide in carefully.
5. The importance of spending time thinking about organization of the office, including attention to the needs of and expectations for office personnel, cannot be overemphasized in this effort. Without them working in earnest to meet the goals of the department, none of the other interventions will ultimately prove successful.

Reflections

1. Staff members must be valued as critical members of the team. Without sensitivity to the role of staff, and their importance in fulfilling the department's mission, a chair puts the entire enterprise at risk for failure. As a colleague once remarked, "If you don't treat the staff well, don't expect to receive important mail three months from now, if ever!"
2. A nonnegotiable skill in managing a department is to avoid public shaming of individuals, especially staff members. The staff is usu-

ally deployed in very public spaces and due to this exposure can be vulnerable to comments and criticisms in a highly visible manner. Defend the right of staff to be treated with respect and dignity at all times.

3. "Acting" follows "believing." Good ideas are only as good as your implementation. Changes in staffing, scheduling, space configurations, decision making, and business practice may each contribute a tiny bit to the culture you want to build. But when added together, their impact increases exponentially.

SEVEN

Jennifer: Vulnerable Reluctant and Anthony: Senior Resistor

"When elephants fight, it is the grass that suffers."

—Kikuyu proverb

You know from research that you have read, as well as experience, that veteran faculty can have a strong impact on a new professor in determining their long-term attitudes toward their position and their school.

When a department becomes dysfunctional, it leaves many individual faculty members in an abyss. This is particularly true of new, nontenured people who are already feeling insecure. These new faculty are faced with a number of hoops to jump through to assure their reappointment and ultimate tenure, including the demonstration of good teaching, service, and publication.

When they are working in a department where there are divisions within the faculty, they often feel that they need to decide whether they should affiliate with one group or another. Or, they might wonder if they should try to stay below the radar. If they are active in trying to establish reputations as hard workers and high producers, this might threaten certain veteran faculty members that are on personnel committees that vote on their reappointment or promotion. All of these concerns are real, and all have played out at one time or another in most universities.

New faculty are easily seduced by negative people, especially if they do not read the power structures correctly and assume these negative faculty have power . . . an image they often portray to new hires.

Even those who are more veteran and tenured are likely to feel discomfort with what is going on. They observe peers with whom they previously had positive relations now making critical remarks about others, making accusations, refusing to do their fair share of work, and trying to manipulate the system.

Many of the new faculty members are Reluctants. They are highly motivated and want to do well. However, they are hesitant about how forthcoming they should be as they try to learn and navigate the culture of the department. For chairs and deans, the Reluctants group is critical. Fence-sitters could easily fall to one side or the other depending on how they are coached and supported.

Like the Committed, the Reluctants are typically skilled and able professionals with much to offer. They came into their jobs with the intention of doing great things . . . of being highly effective teachers of young people, of becoming known in their area of research, of developing a reputation as respected speakers in their field.

No one takes on a position with a plan to be substandard. No one wants to give up on their dreams nor perceive themselves as less effective than other professionals in their field.

Yet the pressure that can be placed on those who strive to excel, or exercise behaviors that are supported by administration, can be overwhelming for many faculty members, particularly when they are working alongside veteran faculty who might become critical of the institution's leaders. Belonging is a basic psychological need, and the idea of not being accepted by fellow department members can be threatening.

As a leader, you realize that those who are relatively young could be with the university for another thirty or more years, long after you retire. They are, to a large extent, your greatest legacy. Hiring strong individuals is one of a leader's most important jobs and it can make the life of the leader much easier if he can focus less on problematic personnel issues and spend more time on long-term change and fulfilling the department's vision.

The fact that they are members of the university community, as well as their overall performance, is a direct result of your ability to hire and then nurture them and help them grow. If their enthusiasm and support is lost, the institution as a whole, and students they have touched, will pay a high price.

CAUGHT BETWEEN A ROCK AND A HARD PLACE

As an example, consider the case of Jennifer. As a fifth-year English professor, Jennifer is on target to continue through year six and ultimately receive tenure. She has scored well above average on teaching evaluations from her students. She has established an acceptable publication record and has received a moderate-sized grant providing external funding for her research interests.

When she came into the department, Jennifer was mentored by Anthony, a long-term, tenured member of the department. Anthony chaired the committee that hired her, and along with Bruce and Marianne, they make up the English faculty for the Secondary Education Department. Depending on which of them happens to be on campus on a given day, members of this group can be found in each other's offices or going to lunch together. While Jennifer has been on staff for five years, Anthony, Bruce, and Marianne have all been together for more than twelve years.

Jennifer often hears them talk about an incident that involved Anthony a number of years earlier. According to the story, Anthony was charged with making inappropriate comments to a young female student. The woman complained to the department chair, and the incident was referred to the Human Resources Office. Supposedly, the student had a friend who witnessed the incident. According to Anthony, the entire story was embellished and he was "set up" because the student had not received as high a grade as she wanted in his course.

Anthony has shared, in numerous conversations, that when this incident occurred he was not recommended for tenure during the year it was scheduled. According to other stories Jennifer has heard over her time in the department, this was but one situation and there have been a number of other complaints about Anthony's teaching and interactions with students. Jennifer realizes she does not know exactly what happened, but she also feels that it has nothing to do with her own status in the department.

Consequently, while aware of the various rumors, she has not given them a lot of thought one way or the other. However, what was obviously embarrassing for Anthony was the fact that a lot of people in the college were aware he was not given tenure when planned.

As the story goes, the union got involved; a lawsuit was threatened, and ultimately a deal was struck. Anthony's tenure period was extended for an additional year. During that time, he was careful to keep his nose clean and ultimately received his tenure. However, the letter ultimately sent by the provost recommending tenure did refer to concerns about his behavior and warned him of the importance of behaving professionally. While happy to receive tenure, Anthony never got over the fact that the incident occurred and felt the appointment letter was a personal insult.

Ever since then, Anthony has been vocal about boneheaded administrators, the stupid decisions that are always being made in the university, and how the members of the administration are out of touch with reality. In some small measure, these comments reflect the phenomenon of "hurt people hurt." In other words, if a person has felt injured, regardless of the validity of the action or comment, he or she will eventually be tempted to enact revenge on the perceived assailant.

Anthony let the dean know during the previous school year that he believed he should be appointed chair of the department. While he has not held this post before, he pointed to his lengthy tenure in the department and his belief that he had the skills to coalesce the divided factions. With the department in such upheaval, the dean did not see Anthony as a realistic replacement. Based on his reputation, he would only further polarize an already divided group.

Jennifer is well aware that Anthony is not widely respected. In fact, it is pretty common knowledge that he is downright despised by many members of the department. While she has avoided making any comments to anyone, she knows that Anthony is seen as self-centered and primarily concerned with meeting his own needs. Students generally speak critically of him, and most members of the department avoid any kind of professional interaction with him because he does not regularly attend meetings or share in the workload.

At the same time, and for reasons she does not understand, Bruce, Marianne, and a handful of other faculty in the department support Anthony. When she is in a group with them, they often talk about what needs to be done and how "they" would handle matters. This often involves criticism of other department members, many of them colleagues that Jennifer respects and that she knows are highly thought of in the university.

Further, the mention of any department member from outside of their group being appointed as the next chair is considered unacceptable. She knows that no one in the group is likely to be placed in the chair position, and at the same time she feels sympathy for anyone who is brave enough to take the position.

As you start your appointment as the new chair, you are conducting meetings with all seventeen members of the faculty. You and Jennifer have had a positive relationship since her hiring. A year ago you team-taught a class together, and you and your wife had Jennifer and her partner to your house for dinner. There is a mutual trust and respect between you. When you meet with her, she asks if she can speak to you in confidence. You assure her that she can do so, and she shares that she feels caught in a very difficult situation.

Jennifer lets you know that she thinks you are the best person to be in this position. She tells you how much she respects you and will support you. However, she also lets you know that she is under a lot of pressure from a handful of faculty members who are already talking about how they will subvert the dean's efforts to put the department back together. They do not believe that the provost would actually dissolve the department, as he threatened, because it is "too big and too important" to the college. You know who the handful is, and she knows that you know who they are, as well. As a result, you do not pursue this particular question any further.

In addition, Jennifer shares that those who are critical resent the fact that you have received the chair appointment instead of Anthony and have talked about passive-aggressive means of making your life difficult: "Wait until his first faculty meeting when none of us show up." "Guess what happens when he needs people to administer the master's exam!"

Jennifer shares that she has avoided participating in these conversations, but in fact she has sat in meetings when some of these comments were made. In addition, because she is in the same subject area as many of the major players, they have made subtle jokes about how she is obligated to them since they were involved in her hiring and may also be involved in decisions related to her reappointment and ultimate tenure recommendation. While they seemingly do this in a joking manner, Jennifer is convinced that they are sending a message.

Jennifer tears up as she tells you that she feels terribly conflicted. Ethically, she would never support efforts to sabotage you or the steps being taken to serve students. At the same time, she knows how difficult it is to find positions like the one she is in. She does not want to lose it, nor does she want to have to uproot her life and start over again.

Following your meeting with Jennifer, you experience a range of emotions. The first is anger. How could professionals act this way? Could people really be this petty? With so much to do, and with such an important responsibility to students, is this really how people choose to spend their time?

As a department member yourself, and having witnessed a lot of what has gone on over the last couple of years, you are not entirely surprised by what Jennifer had to say. And while you would love to call them on the carpet, you know that this would be of little value. You do not have the luxury of conducting a mass termination. Likewise, you cannot allow yourself to stoop to the same kinds of behaviors that they are practicing.

During your weekly meeting with the dean, you share the conversation you had with Jennifer. The two of you agree that neither of you are surprised by what you have heard and that you need to deal with this situation carefully. You also agree that what you do in this matter will likely foreshadow your approach to problem solving as you move forward. Essentially, it will give faculty a good idea of who you are and how you will function as chair.

After a quiet moment the dean says, "You know, as we've started to wade into this we have seen the multiple issues that are at play, the wide variation of personalities, the behaviors that in some cases are childish while in others are just totally unprofessional. The fact that some of them are telling students in their classrooms how to behave professionally while refusing to behave as professionals themselves is really ironic. It's really hard not to bring some of the individuals in and blast them, but then we would be stooping to the same level that we find unacceptable. In addition, let's face it, we both know that doing so would not result in any real positive change.

"As I said, we knew going into this that we had a challenge in front of us and it wasn't going to be easy. Certainly our joint observations would validate this fact. Here's what I think we should do. Let's try to take as rational an approach to this as possible. We've talked about the three psychological needs of fun, power, and love. We've also talked about the way that some of the behaviors we've witnessed fall into behavioral categories such as Passive, Passive-Aggressive, and Aggressive. What else do we know?"

You add, "Yes, I've thought about that, too. And I guess what makes our jobs so hard is that we can't simply go through a checklist of counterproductive behaviors and then come up with an answer that will automatically fix each problem. When we talk about the psychological needs as the causes of their behaviors, and we talk about their actual actions, or the effects of those actions, we know that none of this is linear. It's more like a Venn diagram with overlaps. And the degree of overlapping changes with the issue, the needs of the person, the people involved, and probably a number of other factors we'll never be aware of. Sounds like Mission Impossible! Are we out of our minds?"

The dean chuckles. "Probably. But that's why we get paid the big bucks, right? Look, I think using the psychological needs and behaviors is absolutely the way to go. It gives us a common understanding and language to use when we talk and work together. More importantly, don't forget the three tenets that you developed. We are here to serve students, adhere to civility, and build excellent programs. In the end, we need to keep these beliefs in mind as we look at people and situations. If we do that in an open and transparent way, we can't go wrong."

The dean notes, "So as an example, we know that when we talk about specific people that behave in counterproductive ways, it seems like there is a primary need that isn't being fulfilled. For instance, Anthony certainly doesn't seem to find coming here to be enjoyable. And while he has a few people who are friendly toward him, he's got to be aware that most of the people in the department really don't have a lot of respect for him. So if we are talking about needs, he probably isn't having a lot of fun and he certainly isn't widely loved."

You note, "But when we talk about individuals in relation to the three behaviors, they can behave with passive behavior and/or passive-aggressive behavior and/or all three on a given day. It's more fluid."

"I agree," the dean says. "So let's continue to use the beliefs as guiding principles and also consider their psychological needs and actual behaviors as a frame of reference in how we respond to them."

EXPLANATION OF JENNIFER'S BEHAVIOR

Broadly speaking, Jennifer and her colleagues that have attempted to stay out of department politics will require a great deal of your time as chair. They deserve regular attention in order to ensure that they avoid intimidation or indoctrination by negative faculty members. You and the dean need to counsel them through the difficult times and let them know that they have support. They need to be asked about their concerns and needs regularly and then be responded to as reasonably as possible.

Depending on the dynamics, a small support group might even be convened so they can talk to each other. This group might meet for lunch, off campus, every month or two. The dean might make an outside facilitator available to them, or you or the dean might sit in with them, depending on the interests of the group.

And while you are aware of this, there is also the immediate situation to deal with. The conversation with the dean resonates. You are aware that transparency and consistency are crucial. In considering what has happened, you realize there are a number of issues you need to deal with:

1. Jennifer has the right to work in an environment that is free of threat from anyone: administration, faculty, or students. Any consideration for continuing in her faculty position or future promotions should be based on contractual guidelines and not politics.
2. The behaviors that Anthony and his cabal are involved in will only deepen the existing wounds and prevent the department from ever healing.
3. Confronting Anthony and his supporters could be beneficial in terms of letting them know that you and the dean are aware of their plans; however, confronting them could also put Jennifer in an extremely awkward position with other faculty members.

MORE EFFECTIVE MEANS TO ENGAGE JENNIFER

As chair, your first responsibility is always to the students in the program. This goes back to the three beliefs you have identified. In this particular situation, the students are insulated. Jennifer is an effective teacher, and the politics that are taking place really should not affect them.

Since you feel the students are protected, your next priority is to your faculty and the need for safety and civility. In this case, Jennifer's vulnerability is not necessarily just a perception on her part, but could be a reality if Anthony and his supporters were in positions where they could hurt her—for instance, if they were on any personnel committees. Likewise, they could also make life more difficult on a daily basis in subject-level meetings and in normal social interactions, such as in the hallways and in other meetings.

As you weigh these concerns along with the need to maintain the confidentiality you assured Jennifer of when you spoke, you realize that you should share your game plan with her before you take any action. Your relationship with her is a primary concern. You absolutely must maintain the trust she showed by coming to you and talking about her concerns about Anthony and company. A well-known maxim applies here: Trust is so hard to gain but so easy to lose.

Trust is an absolute. Whether peers agree or disagree with routine daily decisions you make is much less important than your rationale and behavior in carrying out those decisions.

Meeting with Jennifer provides you with an opportunity to share your plans and ask her opinion. First, you let her know how much you appreciated her coming to you. You inform her that you have some ideas on how to move forward, but that your relationship with her is important and you do not want to take any action without first making sure that she is comfortable with what you propose.

> You: *Thanks for coming in again. I have been thinking about the conversation that we had at my house, and I wanted to talk with you before I move forward on this.*

> Jennifer: *I appreciate your listening to me, but really, I don't want to start anything.*

Jennifer's response validates her concern that repercussions might occur if any of the Resistors believed that she was talking with the chair.

> You: *I want you to know that I am committed to your being treated in a respectful and professional manner. And I heard your concerns when you spoke with me at my house when we had dinner recently. Now, I have a question for you: What do you want?*

Jennifer deserves reassurance. However, when giving it be very careful not to make promises you cannot keep. Do not promise that her reappointment will go through without a problem. You are not on the committee and cannot speak for them. Further, you do not want word getting around the college that you made such a commitment when you are not in a position to do so.

Also, asking her what she wants is a CRITICAL QUESTION that you will use often when talking with others. It will require people to think explicitly about the concern at hand and what they would like to ultimately see occur as a result of your conversations. It also gives you a potential goal. Expect this simple question to cause Jennifer to pause. Do not fill in the gap if she stops to think; instead, allow her time to process and respond.

Jennifer: *Well, I guess the bottom line is that I'm concerned about what is going on and the way people have treated others and . . .*

You: *I hear you and I appreciate that, but what I want to know is, what do you want?*

Jennifer: *Hmm . . . okay. I guess, well, I guess I just don't want to have to worry about getting a fair shake when it comes to my reappointment and tenure. I don't want Anthony or some of the other people to mess up my chances of staying here. I know that doesn't sound very professional or highly academic, but that's really what I'm afraid of.*

You: *I fully understand, and I want you to know that I will not allow anything you have shared with me to cause any problems for you in terms of getting fair consideration. As we talked about at my house, there are issues and behaviors going on here that are not acceptable. Neither you, nor any other faculty, should feel intimidated by anyone, whether it's someone in the administration or the teaching faculty or anyone else.*

I have a lot of respect for you and want you to know that you have my support. I do plan to call Anthony in for a talk, but I will not be bringing up your name, nor will I tell him that anyone even came in to speak to me. At this point, I am going to just ask him to give me his thoughts on the state of the department and ask for his suggestions and support.

I'm doing this in hope of building some bridges and trying to see if we can get him to be more positive.

Jennifer's grimace when you say this tells you what she is probably thinking. However, starting out in a positive manner with Anthony is a necessary step and is going to lay an important groundwork for you.

You: *If after we meet he continues to act in ways that are destructive, I will deal with him then. However, it's important to me that we start out this way and give him a chance to respond. And it also keeps you out of the picture.*

The other thing I wanted to tell you is that you have one job to worry about and that is to be a good, productive professor. I'm going to be vigilant about making sure the personnel process is conducted in a clean and fair manner and your reviews are objective and by the book. Likewise, rest assured that the "powers above" are already well aware of the environment here, and I have made sure that they are also well aware of the work you have done, so you do not need to be fearful. Okay?

Jennifer: *Okay. I appreciate your listening and following through. Hopefully, we can begin to move forward in the department.*

Jennifer has given you her specific concerns, and you have reassured her that you plan to address them. Following this conversation you begin to plan the steps you are going to take to make sure reassurance and reality come together.

First, you realize that job security is the foremost issue on Jennifer's mind. You have let her know that you can certainly understand her concerns and would feel the same way. Next you shared with her what you will not do. You will not mention her to Anthony or any of his supporters since you do not want to put her in an awkward position or let anyone know about your conversation.

Next, you outlined your plan on moving forward. You let her know that you want to be sure that she will be given fair consideration when she is reviewed for reappointment and tenure. In addition, you have let her know that you went out of your way to talk specifically about her with the dean and provost.

In order to continue with your next steps, you are going to use the "informal network" that exists in all organizations. You need to get to your colleagues on the faculty who you know are professional and fair-minded. You will let them know that you need people who are highly respected to help out. They have to be willing to volunteer to run for seats on the personnel committee, curriculum committee, and other structures in the department where it is important to ensure smooth operations as well as make sure that all faculty are treated fairly.

While you do not need to be specific with Jennifer as to who those people are, you will likely start with the faculty members who originally came to you and asked you to take the chair position. While you do not expect that it will take much prodding, you realize that the only way to pull the department back together is if everyone shares in meaningful work that will move you forward. This not only causes them to be more vested in your immediate efforts, but it also helps them develop the skills needed to assist in the rebuilding effort.

You have also taken one other very important step—you have outlined your plan to establish a positive first step forward with Anthony. This is important. You must always think ahead about what is likely to happen in the future and whether you have done everything necessary to try to work in a proactive manner to resolve a situation in a way that will be win-win for all involved.

In this particular case, if Anthony does not wish to cooperate in this effort, you want it documented that you made a reasonable effort to include him in working together cooperatively. Should Anthony decide to file a complaint against you in the future, it is to your benefit to be able to refer to these conversations and have copies of follow-up emails providing evidence of your efforts and Anthony's unwillingness to participate.

Now that you have outlined your plan to Jennifer and received her agreement, you ask her to keep you informed if any further issues should arise.

MORE EFFECTIVE MEANS TO ENGAGE ANTHONY

At this point you have an understanding of Jennifer's concerns, and your next consideration is engaging Anthony. You have made a commitment to keep Jennifer out of the line of fire. At the same time, you realize that doing nothing is only going to result in Anthony and his supporters continuing with their counterproductive behaviors, and you cannot let this happen. In fact, this malaise is really one of the biggest issues the department has to deal with and is at the core of the larger problems that exist.

In determining where to start, you think about the process of "progressive discipline." This concept suggests that when you are dealing with a potential discipline problem, your first efforts should be minimally invasive. The idea is to try to exact change without having to take extreme actions that would be painful or costly to those involved. The purpose is to fix the problem while saving face for all involved and maintaining support. For instance, if an employee were regularly late coming to work, their supervisor might have a number of options.

At the initial level, when dealing with a minor infraction, simpler and less intrusive actions should be taken, such as a conversation outlining your concern and what you expect. At the harshest level, if the behavior is repeated a number of times, the employee might be suspended, fined, or reprimanded. Any of these actions would likely result in the anger and resentment of the employee, and, in the long run, could damage their commitment to the organization and their job duties. You decide as you prepare to meet with Anthony that any concerns can be handled at the initial level.

While these steps are progressive, based on a minor to moderate problem, progressive discipline does not preclude you from "skipping" a step or steps if a violation is more extreme. For instance, if any faculty or staff member has engaged in physical violence, drug or alcohol abuse, or a number of other more egregious behaviors, you would likely skip the first steps and immediately go to the third or final. While you do not anticipate taking any action against Anthony at this time, and hope to avoid it in the long term, you tell yourself that having an understanding of this process may be worthwhile for future reference.

You have invited Anthony to meet with you, and you make a point of making eye contact with him and shaking his hand when he enters your office. You let him know that you are feeling a great deal of responsibility with the duties you have taken on and share that you are trying to get feedback from faculty members that will be helpful in moving forward. You ask Anthony for his suggestions on what can be done to help the department move forward.

You: *Anthony, thanks for coming in. How is your semester going?*

Anthony: *Well, fine. Everything seems to be going okay.*

You: *Anthony, as we both know, the department has been a mess the last few years. I have no interest in getting involved in the politics and finger pointing that have occurred, and I'm sure you don't either. I am hopeful that we can all work together to put an end to it and move forward in a cooperative and civil manner.*

And so you know, I am having this conversation with everyone. But I particularly plan to lean on senior professors in the department for support. This has been our home for a long time, and I feel like we are the ones that need to take leadership at a time like this.

At this point you are only trying to be positive. You have laid out your agenda in a low-key, cooperative manner. You have tried to make him comfortable by acknowledging his position as a senior professor who has the capacity to influence the efforts that need to be made.

No one could argue with the goals you are trying to accomplish. Hopefully, Anthony is nodding his head in a positive manner or saying a few words to acknowledge his agreement.

You: *As a senior member of the department, give me your thoughts on where we are and what you think we need to do to pull ourselves out of this funk.*

Give Anthony a chance to respond. There may be points you could challenge, but don't. You are trying to build bridges right now, and disagreeing on a point is not likely to help you reach your ultimate goal.

In addition, listen carefully to what he has to say. As a senior member, he might share insights that will help you better understand his views and behaviors. While you may not like him personally, Anthony may have valuable ideas that can help you gain insights on why he behaves as he does, and what you can do to improve his role in the department.

Also, be sure when you respond to him that you restate some of the important points he makes. Be particularly certain to restate any suggestions that he provides and how you might be able to implement some of them if possible.

You: *I really appreciate your insights and suggestions. Your idea of having "share sessions" once a month, where faculty can share a strategy with others in the department, is a great idea. Would you be willing to work with me on identifying some people to set that up?*

Working together may help build a bridge and begin to develop some trust between you. Share sessions would be simple to set up, and you could provide him recognition for his efforts.

It is also important to let him know about some of your plans as well as the nonnegotiables that concern you:

You: *As I said, the share sessions are terrific. The one other thing I'm trying to get a handle on is some of the backbiting that has gone on in the past. I know it has already started, and I want to put a stop to it as soon as possible. I'm a member of the family here, too. I know that many faculty members think that a faculty member loses any common sense they may have when they become a chair or go into administration, but this isn't a career goal of mine. I will be coming back to the department at some point in the future, but right now I need the support of my colleagues. Do you have any thoughts on steps I should take to get the negative comments to stop and get the support of the faculty?*

This is not a comfortable conversation to have with Anthony. However, there is no doubt you are going to have to deal with the issue sooner or later. The longer you wait, the more it is going to fester. Getting it on the table now, and approaching it in a constructive manner, provides a number of benefits.

First, using the progressive discipline approach, you are at the very bottom rung of the ladder in dealing with this environment that has been building up over several years. Second, you are giving Anthony a chance to get on board and be part of the solution rather than continuing to be a part of the problem. Will he take it? Probably not, but you need to be positive and hopeful. Once in a while you will be surprised.

The other thing that you have done is let Anthony know in a non-threatening manner that you are aware of some of the behaviors that are going on to undermine you, and you are sending a message that you do not plan to tolerate them.

He does not know if you are aware that he has taken leadership in some of the major issues that exist in the department or not. And at this point, that is not important. What he is aware of is that you too have pipelines in the department, and there is going to be a strong likelihood that word will get back to you of destructive efforts that may take place. Finally, it would be good to conclude the conversation with the same question you asked Jennifer: "What do you want?"

The chances are good that Anthony will talk about peace and cohesion in the department. And while you may be sitting there thinking about how hypocritical that sounds, based on his past behaviors, it provides you with a frame of reference for future conversations.

You may also want to ask Anthony about his perceptions of how the department got to this point in the first place. However, and this is critical, you do not want to dwell on the past, and any discussion on history should be brief. You have to let him know that you are asking each faculty member what he or she would be willing to do to help repair the damage that has occurred between many of the faculty. This too provides you with something to refer to in later conversations, if appropriate.

Finally, you also will want to ask him if there is anything you can do to help him as you work together to move the department forward. Take notes and be sure to send a thank you email and include what was shared.

At this point there is no "disciplining" going on. The overtures you are making are in the spirit of problem solving, and this is an initial action that will cause no harm, but hopefully will change some existing behaviors. No mention is being made of Jennifer since you will not violate that trust. Presently, the idea is to be positive, to listen and respond where possible, and to establish your interest in moving the department forward with the support of all members.

You have invited him to see your interest in working together in a constructive manner, and this is all you can do. You have done everything that you reasonably can at this point, and the decision to accept or reject what you have offered is up to Anthony.

Will this effort likely result in significant, public changes in attitudes and behaviors? Obviously, you will not know immediately. However, it does do a number of very important things: First, it reinforces that your style is to meet personally with faculty members to deal with concerns, rather than doing so through emails or phone calls. Second, it allows you to reiterate on a one-to-one basis what you have been saying in your newsletters and small group meetings about where you want to see the department go and how you will behave in your role.

Third, it has provided everyone with a chance to share their personal concerns. In other words, faculty members cannot say that people in leadership have ignored or failed to listen to them. In addition, you may learn some important things that you can implement to improve the wellness of the department. By listening and acting while giving credit to the faculty who share their suggestions, you get a chance to build trust.

You have also established understandings for future reference. In other words, you have shared your vision and expectations about the three beliefs and other matters of common concern. Likewise, faculty members have had a chance to share their expectations with you. You need to let each faculty member know that if they observe you behaving in ways that are inconsistent with your belief statements and what you have said, they are welcome to make you aware of it. They should be assured that feedback will always be welcomed and both given and taken in a constructive spirit.

JENNIFER AND ANTHONY: OBSERVATIONS

Jennifer and Anthony have provided you with your initiation to leadership of this very dysfunctional department. During your recent conversation with the dean, she pointed out that this is going to be an important time. Everyone will be looking at how you handle a situation that is personnel related. Will you be calm or will you get angry? How will you communicate, through emails or face-to-face? Will you have your "pets" on the faculty who are favored? Will you be consistent in how you deal with people? Do those three belief statements really mean anything, or are they just fluff? Essentially, will you "walk the talk?" And the answer to this, quite simply, is that only time will tell.

Following your meetings with Jennifer, Anthony, and other faculty, you and the dean have your weekly meeting. When you talk about this case you share that you have been faithful to the three beliefs as a frame of reference.

In terms of psychological needs, Jennifer has been assured of her basic safety. She knows that her work will be evaluated based on its merit and that she does not need to fear political retribution from faculty members whose opinions differ from her own. While you cannot guarantee her need for love or affiliation will be met by Anthony and some of his supporters, you can assure her that you will make sure that she and the other faculty members who are working each day to be effective contributors will be protected.

The dean points out that in considering the needs of Anthony and some of those who support him, both of you recognize that their present passive-aggressive behavior has been a continuing problem. Further, you know that some of them have stepped over the line of passive-aggressive into aggressive behaviors. Subtle bullying has taken place in the past, as witnessed by the comments made to Jennifer about her reappointment.

And while you tend to think about Jennifer as the potential victim in all of this, it is also important to think about Anthony and some of his followers. While their behaviors may be distasteful, you need to ask yourself how they got to this point. Each one needs to be considered individually since each will have his or her own story.

In Anthony's case, you have offered him the same psychological safety net that you provided to Jennifer. You have made it clear that you are aware of some of his actions in the past, but you are willing to put them aside if he is willing to join with you in moving forward in a positive manner. For Anthony, the question will be whether he gains greater gratification for his power and affiliation needs through his more destructive behaviors.

The one-on-one meetings that you have might be one way to identify the motivations and behaviors of individuals. Asking them their perceptions of the department as a whole can be enlightening. Asking them for their perceptions of their own effectiveness can also provide some insights. Asking the question "What do you want?" forces respondents to focus. And once they articulate their want or need, it provides you a starting point for conversation or action, if appropriate.

Reflecting on this, you have decided that while educators typically have a great deal of latitude in how they conduct themselves, aggressive behaviors will not be negotiable as long as you are in this position. Yelling, lying, bullying, and some of the other behaviors that have occurred in the past will not be tolerated if they come to your attention. Regardless of who initiates it, an appropriate response will take place. Ignoring such behaviors will only perpetuate them.

You let the dean know that you want to give everyone a fresh start and do not want to get involved in past actions. This is why you decided to have initial meetings with faculty on an individual basis. Everyone will be asked the same questions, and you will do your best to treat people as equitably as possible.

Likewise, she notes that there have been a handful of situations that you should also be aware of in case similar situations should reoccur. She shares that if repeat offenses of serious problems arise, they may need to be handled in a more stringent manner.

Personal Reflection

The Reluctants are critically important to you as a chair. They are typically good instructors and contributors who have tried to stay out of the fray. However, when departments remain dysfunctional for long periods, they can become frustrated with a lack of progress and become cynical, feeling there is no real hope for the future.

Like the Committed group, they see the lack of participation by Resistors and begin to wonder why they should be attending meetings and working above and beyond what is necessary when Resistors are leaving early, failing to participate in meetings and committees, and refusing to share in the workload.

For many, this becomes even more frustrating when they consider that the negotiated contract assures that the Resistors will often continue to receive larger raises because of where they fall on the salary schedule, while their productivity spirals downward. As one Reluctant shared with you, "They have too much time on their hands."

You hope that your efforts as a new chair will begin to provide faculty and staff with some optimism that things will in fact be different. Working in a contractual environment does not allow you to give bonuses or trips or other perks when people do things right; however, you are able to recognize people for good work. It is especially important to pat someone on the back, give a word of thanks, and send a congratulatory note on letterhead with copies to the dean (and other administrators, as appropriate) when someone has done something above and beyond the norm.

When you recall your early years in the department, you are reminded of faculty celebrating their time together when they gathered in meetings. People would take turns bringing in snacks, and members would joke and look forward to going out to lunch together. While that has been lost, you realize that in the long run, changing the culture is the real goal that you need to work toward.

You also realize that the slow deterioration that got you where you are today is not going to be turned around in a few semesters. "Turning the

Titantic" comes to mind. This is going to take time. It is going to mean that a number of efforts will need to take place, such as difficult but honest discussions outlining specific concerns and expectations, aimed at the rehabilitation of people who are acting unprofessionally; possibly refusing tenure to individuals who are not willing to work together in a collaborative manner to serve students; and moving assignments and schedules.

Perhaps one of the most common errors of new leaders is their effort to please everyone. Efforts to support Committed and Reluctant faculty may be responded to critically and with skepticism by Resistors. Leaders need to understand that this behavior is not an indicator of their failure to be effective, but rather the inability of Resistors to find happiness and satisfaction in their own lives. When you think back to the teachers that you have known over the years who were happy, positive, and effective in their classrooms, you realize that typically those same people were happy, positive, and effective in their personal lives as well.

Likewise, when you consider those faculty that students complain about, who did not want to go the extra mile to do quality work or support student-related activities, and are not happy or fun to be around, they are the same ones that receive the poorest evaluations from students and that fellow faculty avoid.

Reluctants are much too valuable to lose. Not only are they important for the service they provide to students today and in the future, they also will become future leaders that will be a source for rebuilding. They are an important resource to be prized, and every reasonable effort should be made to involve them in the rebuilding of the department.

EIGHT

Mary: Passive Resistor

"If someone has an issue, talk to them. Don't make comments in meetings, in the parking lot, or through emails to the chair."

—A professor

Analyzing why people behave as they do is not the purpose of this book. Volumes have been written on the subject and are readily available. What we do know is that the field of education is populated by a large number of creative and talented people. Most of them are dedicated and committed to serving students. At the same time, there is a small minority of individuals who do not share that commitment and are more focused on meeting their own desires, even if it is at the expense of those same students.

This observation was verified by the professor who was in a challenging discussion with his department head and said, "Your job as a department chair is to take care of the faculty first," and truly meant it.

Individuals who behave in ways that appear to be contrary to the mission of the university and who look for ways to create dissension rather than problem-solve are labeled here as Resistors.

Unfortunately, the academy as an enterprise is uniquely poised to allow Resistors to stay off of the radar and not contribute to fulfilling the mission of the university or the goals of the college and department. By avoiding conflict, by not engaging in difficult conversations, and by failing to document expectations and follow through with accountability, universities allow Resistors to flourish.

This occurs in many different ways: letting a faculty member only teach his classes and come to meetings at a time convenient to him rather than act in the best interest of students or programs; avoiding conversations that demarcate unprofessional conduct; or enabling "victim-bully" behavior, where an individual claims that she is the one being victimized

71

by being held accountable to fulfill professional expectations, such as attending department meetings at the prescribed days and times, serving as a representative on college-wide committees, sitting on master's and doctoral committees, or monitoring examinations.

One of the tried and true methods for leaders to address these infractions is to apply two key principles: consistency and time. By using consistent responses to inappropriate behaviors, the leader reinforces those behaviors that are "in bounds" and hopes to extinguish those that are "out of bounds." This consistency, applied to all members of the department in the same manner, establishes a common understanding of responsibilities and expectations.

An important second factor is the commitment to maintain these consistent responses over time. Negative behaviors are reinforced for many people by a common enemy, *fatigue*. Leaders would prefer that negative behaviors disappear so that they do not have to engage in conflict, such as having an uncomfortable conversation with a faculty member. By not being consistent over time, leaders inadvertently reinforce bad behaviors that, once established, are extremely hard to eradicate.

The Resistors are the best examples of this. They tend to look for opportunities that will allow them to pursue their own interests. These may be a result of administrative turnover, inconsistent leadership, bullying, or a myriad of other potential sources.

What follows is a case study of Mary, a Resistor on the faculty.

Mary is an associate professor in her ninth year in the department. Her background is in science, and she had six years of public school classroom experience prior to earning her doctorate and joining the department.

Resistors in your department can be found in a few different subgroups. As noted previously, three members of the English area, Anthony, Bruce, and Marianne, have been active in trying to undermine the efforts of leadership. While there are two members in the science area, Mary's colleague, Ronald, is generally not supportive of her and in fact is actually a proactive, Committed member of the department.

School has just started, and you are involved in typical opening-week activities. When you arrive on Wednesday morning you turn on your computer and see a copy of an email written by Mary to all members of the department. The email reads as follows:

Dear Colleagues: Well, it looks like we've been had . . . again! I taught my first science lab last night and there were 16 students present. That is a very full lab. And that would have been all right if the lab was equipped to handle them. The administration promised us new lab equipment, and I was shocked to walk in and find the same old materials were still present. I know that other departments were also told that there would be classroom renovations and new equipment provided but when I walked down the hallways I did not see ANY-

THING different! Just a word of warning to everyone . . . be careful about believing everything you hear!

As you read this you just shake your head in wonder. In all your years in education you have never witnessed an economic recession as painful as the one that you are now in. Public schools throughout the country have been furloughing veteran teachers. At your own university a hiring freeze has taken place and restrictions have been placed on purchasing and travel. But the good news is that no one has lost their job.

Prior to the end of the last school year, a lengthy memo went out to the entire department on this same topic. The assistant dean outlined that with the crunch in the budget statewide, funding for building renovations and equipment updates was being put on hold. He also noted that the hold would probably be in place for one to two semesters, and the provost indicated that he was confident it would not be longer than that.

The assistant dean also shared this same information with the Faculty Council at the end of the last academic year, and the information was printed in the April minutes of the council meeting that went out to all faculty. In line with your commitment to keeping things transparent, you know you have to respond to this with a communication that goes out to the entire department. At the same time, while you do not appreciate the combative tone of the email, you know you have to maintain your self-discipline and respond to Mary in a tempered, professional manner.

After some thought, you decide it is best to deal with Mary directly. Mary's action, while frustrating, is not new. You have seen this kind of behavior from her several times over the years, and since this is the start of your assignment as chair, you do not want her to continue this kind of subterfuge during or after your appointment. If the department is going to heal, it has to stop. You also realize that this must be handled quickly. The email has gone out and people will be digesting it. You need to communicate with the entire faculty as soon as reasonably possible, but you decide that you need to deal with Mary first.

As you reflect on what has occurred thus far, it is apparent to you that Mary's behavior falls into the category of aggressive negative behavior. You are well aware that Mary likes to conduct much of her aggressiveness from afar. Her charges are always through email. She never does it on a one-to-one basis with those with whom she disagrees. Ironically, in faculty meetings she often makes comments about how everyone needs to work together, and yet, she has also become the master of taking "potshots" at leadership when she gets the chance.

Mary needs to know that she has to take responsibility for her actions. Leadership in the past has typically ignored her comments, and as a result she has taken this as license to continue.

If Mary is going to make charges of this sort, she has to know that she will be held accountable. As a result, you email Mary and let her know that you have concerns with her communication and would like to meet with her on Friday morning when she comes in to teach her class. Mary responds and makes it clear she does not want to meet with you.

> Mary: *I don't understand why we need to meet. As I noted in my memo to the department, this is a departure from what we have done in the past. Am I being disciplined now for communicating with my colleagues?*

> You: *Not at all. But there is a lot of information related to this topic that was not communicated in your memo to the faculty, and I want to be sure that the two of us have a common understanding of what led up to this charge. Since there is a lot more to this, it would be much easier to meet in person and talk about it rather than going back and forth in emails.*

Your first impulse is to ask: "Don't you think that all members of the faculty should have all the available facts?" However, you know that doing this is likely to result in a lengthy string of more emails. Consequently, you decide to avoid discussion and simply reiterate that you would like to meet in person.

> Mary: *Well we do have a right as faculty members to communicate our concerns to one another, don't we? I hope you aren't suggesting that I don't have the right to share things. After all, we do need to be open about things. If that's the case, I'm not going to be happy about this, and I know that the rest of the faculty won't be either.*

Mary is doing her best to deflect responsibility for what she has written and shared. In addition to failing to respond to your request, she is sending the not-so-subtle message that it is not just her that you are "threatening," but the entire faculty. Recognizing that Mary is doing her best to avoid the substance of the conversation, you realize that you cannot allow this to happen. If you do, she will use this approach any time a future situation arises. Further, if she believes she can do it successfully whenever she decides to, you know you will lose any control of her entirely and her counterproductive behaviors will persist.

At this time, you need to make two points. The first is that you are in a position of authority and while it is not something you plan to exercise often, you will when you feel it is appropriate. Second, the situation itself needs to be clarified. Obviously, this is not going to happen over email.

You want to meet with Mary to go over the history of the issue and how the present decision was ultimately made. It is important to see Mary face-to-face. This is not what she wants to do, but she needs to know that it is going to be the likely result if she insists on using electronic means to communicate with the entire department in order to create dissension.

Mary's communication also raises a red flag that needs to be responded to immediately. Her comment that faculty need permission to email is obviously absurd. However, life in the department over the last few years has been characterized by its share of absurdity. Mary is doing her best to shift her bullying behaviors to you.

Your response to her needs to make it clear that you want to meet in person. You also need to let her know, in writing, that she and all department members have a right to email anything they want, and her statement to you is absolutely not accurate. It is important to always think ahead. If for any reason Mary decides to bring this up in a meeting with other faculty, you want to be sure that you have made it clear that the interpretation was hers, not yours. In Mary's world, your failure to respond to her comment could be taken as consent and used against you. It is time to reiterate that you are not taking away any faculty member's right to communicate and you do expect her to meet with you. This needs to be said respectfully and briefly.

> You: *Mary, I don't feel you are hearing what I'm saying to you. I absolutely do not agree with your statements about faculty not having the right to communicate. Certainly, people have the right to share their views and comments. What I am saying is that I believe it would be in the best interest of everyone involved to be dealing with all of the information, not just snippets or one person's understanding. I have some information on the background of this decision that you might not be aware of. Likewise, you might have some that I am not aware of.*
>
> *Before I send out an email to the faculty in response to your comments, I want to make sure we have shared what we both know. If we decide to agree or disagree with the decision after that, certainly we can do so in a professional manner. Please contact my assistant and let me know when you can meet tomorrow. I look forward to seeing you.*

Your next step is important. Mary is not going to be happy about meeting with you in person, but realizes that it is now necessary. Regardless of her feelings, it is important that your dialogue with her is centered on facts and data.

On entering your office, Mary gives you a broad smile. You make eye contact and shake her hand. She comments, "*So am I being taken to the woodshed?*" You are surprised to hear her say this. Obviously, she knows that what she did would not be acceptable to you, yet she did it anyway. This at least clarifies any question you might have in your own mind about whether Mary was conscious of what she was doing.

You assure her that going to the woodshed is not the purpose of the meeting. You reiterate that you have two concerns. The first is to clarify the decisions and communications that had occurred regarding the budget. The second, larger one, is to stop perpetuating actions that have the potential to cause further dissension in the department.

Mary assures you that peace in the department is a major concern of hers as well and the last thing she wants to do is cause further problems.

"Huh?" you ask yourself, but don't say aloud.

After a pause, you realize that engaging in further conversation on this is probably not going to be helpful, and it's best to stick to your purpose:

> You: *Mary, I read and re-read the email you sent out to everyone. Look, I want to reiterate what I said to you about my respecting your right, and the right of everyone in the department, to exchange points of view, concerns, or even complaints. But as professors we, more than any other group I can think of, need to observe the principle of informed decision making. We all deserve to have as many of the pertinent facts available to us as possible.*
>
> *Here are copies of three different communications that the assistant dean sent out at the end of last year and during the summer regarding the economic crunch the university is in and how it affects our department. They point out very clearly that this has been an ongoing issue, but the university remains steadfast in fulfilling the commitments that have been made once the financial crisis is under control. The union has made it clear that they wish to keep people employed rather than have layoffs. As a result, at least for now, it's people over equipment and renovations.*
>
> *Is there something more that you know that I don't? If I misinterpreted this somehow, I'm certainly willing to try to fix any errors.*

Mary has been quiet to this point. She waits for you to finish, and then shares that while she knew that this matter had been reviewed, she did not really believe that it applied in your department.

> Mary: *Yes, I know all this took place, but still, this need has existed for a long time and we should have had new labs and equipment a long time ago.*
>
> You: *You are probably correct about that, Mary. However, I don't pretend to know the history of the budget and how decisions were made over the past years. If you are interested, I can contact the business official and ask him to sit down with you and give you that information. But in the meantime, this is where we stand and it appears we are going to have to wait for a while.*
>
> Mary, with a frown on her face: *No, I guess we'll just have to wait.*
>
> You: *Mary, I appreciate your coming in to talk about this, and I'd like to ask you a question. What do you want for the department?*
>
> Mary: *I'm not sure what you mean. If you are talking about the problems that exist, no one wants us to all get along more than I do.*
>
> You: *I'm sure that's true. But let me ask you another question. Think about the email you sent out and some of the charges you made and words you used. Do you think your actions will bring people together and produce a more positive environment?*
>
> Mary: *Well, in a way. I mean, it's a problem for our whole department.*
>
> You: *Perhaps. But I have to tell you, in my own observation, I was well aware of what led to this, and the combative nature of what you said made me feel like we were just going deeper into the hole that many of our colleagues have fallen into. For me what you wrote had exactly the opposite effect. Instead of building*

a positive climate, it just accentuates more negativity. Further, be assured that when you send out an email like that, everyone around here is going to see it. The dean, assistant dean, maybe even the provost. If you are trying to cause further conflict between the department and their offices, it's only going to continue to reinforce the reputation we have been trying to change.

In the meantime, to assure that there is no misunderstanding, I plan to send a note out to the faculty outlining our discussion and include copies of the materials they received last semester from the assistant dean. In fact, to be sure we are in agreement as to what we have discussed, I will send a copy of the memo to you first to confirm that what I am saying accurately portrays our discussion.

I really appreciate your coming in. And like I said, this isn't aimed at anything other than working together to share information and being transparent about issues that affect everyone. Please feel free to contact me in the future if anything comes up; I'd be glad to meet with you.

Following your goodbyes, you immediately write a memo to faculty summarizing the discussion that you had with Mary and attach a copy of the various communications on this topic that had previously gone out. It is wise to do this while everything is fresh in your mind. And since you are sending it to Mary to review first, you want her to see that it was done right after your discussion took place and that it is accurate. This also makes her aware that you follow up on what you say you are going to do and do not procrastinate.

You should get your email out to Mary as soon as possible, within the hour if you can (be sure to proofread it—twice). Ask Mary to review it and call you by the next morning if she has anything to add. After that, send the email to faculty. Let them know you understand Mary's concerns, that you met with her to discuss them, and you reviewed how the decision was made.

Be transparent and matter of fact. Note Mary's concerns (she has proofread the email so she will not be surprised) as well as your own understanding. This is a first in your new tenure as chair. It provides an opportunity to show how you will handle sensitive issues. With time and consistency, people will develop a better understanding of who you are as a leader, what you stand for, and how you will conduct business. They may not always like it, but they will not be surprised.

The reality is that many people love drama in the workplace. Suggesting that professionals are above a bit of soap opera is not realistic. Whisperers, saboteurs, and defamers can all be found lurking about the hallways, parking lots, and offices of most organizations, and universities are no exception. Mary is wont to orchestrate such drama, and it is important to bring such instances into the open to be exposed for what they are.

Dealing in facts and minimizing the sensitive dynamics around a concern sends a message to Mary and her supporters that important decisions affecting the entire department will be shared with the all members of the department. And further, those decisions will consider facts and viewpoints from all sides.

While Mary's email was definitely aggressive and aimed at criticizing others, she is also a regular member of all three categories of the Axis of Negative Behaviors. When confronted with facts, she commonly references "the good of the students" and her strong desire to "see the department get back together." While this may sound noble, and Mary says the right words, her actions do not always align with what she says. She regularly wants to be given the first choices of classes to teach, rooms to use, and students to be enrolled in her courses. So while she may believe her comments are noble, they ring hollow to those who know her well.

While Mary's behavior is discouraging, it is relatively easy to anticipate. She has been in the department for nine years. Since you have more seniority, you have observed her since she arrived and are well aware of her bullying practices.

Like most bullies, Mary hates being confronted with facts. They have little room in her world. She is always looking to make her own life easier but couches her requests as being in the best interests of the students. The best way of dealing with Mary in the present is to anticipate her actions and examine her requests carefully, since inevitably they will be aimed at benefiting her personally.

Being a realist, you understand the challenges that Mary brings to you and the department. At the same time, you have made a personal commitment to yourself and the dean that you are not going to give up on anyone. As a result, your demeanor with Mary, as with all members of the department, must always remain respectful and professional.

However, it must also be honest and transparent. You know that Mary will not be able to have the perfect schedule that she would like. Other faculty members want to instruct some of the same classes and use the same rooms. The department has been on a rotation over the years with everyone taking turns in these areas, and you cannot accede to one person's wishes over the wishes of others.

Sitting down with Mary, along with a copy of the master schedule, is one step you should take. Another useful strategy is to have other faculty members who would be affected by Mary's request also sit in the meeting with the two of you. The chances are good Mary will not be comfortable with this kind of transparency, but letting her know that you want to be open about decisions affecting multiple faculty is hard to argue with.

There are no big secrets regarding who will be teaching which classes, and Mary needs to see how they are being distributed and feel welcome to ask questions. In addition, to show your desire to be supportive, you should check with other departments to see if there are courses available that Mary would be qualified to teach. For instance, several departments teach courses in curriculum, evaluation, and diversity. If these are of interest to Mary, and another department has sections that need covering, she could teach outside of the department. This might make her more productive, and hopefully, happier.

EXPLANATION OF MARY'S BEHAVIORS

By being primarily Passive-Aggressive, Mary has learned that strategies like emails filled with innuendo and finger pointing are effective ways of maintaining instability in the department. After dealing with new chairs every year or two who are sometimes unaware of the department's history, Mary has been better able to get her own way when requesting teaching and room assignments.

As far as meeting her needs, actions like sending out emails that are unsettling and then making a remark about being called to the woodshed show that she knew exactly what she was doing. Mary cloaks her desire to get her way by believing she is a hero to other faculty. Unfortunately, her lack of self-awareness allows this persona to perpetuate.

In terms of fulfilling her need for power, Mary believes her effort to have the choice of courses to teach is indicative of how serious she takes her role as an instructor. As she sees it, if she teaches these courses, rather than other faculty members, students are going to be much better served and therefore validate her. In the meantime, faculty who will be negatively affected if her wishes are granted see her behavior as primarily self-serving.

MORE EFFECTIVE MEANS TO ENGAGE MARY

Some people "get it" and some do not. In Mary's case, you need to make every effort to deal with her professionally and try to curb some of her aggressive and destructive behaviors. How much you share with many initially must be considered. Sharing all of your perceptions of her behaviors would likely result in her totally rejecting you and diminish any possibility of working with her cooperatively in the future. A more gradual approach in which you appear to agree with her self-perceptions of professionalism might create the best results.

An old saying goes, "First you stroke them, and then you poke them." Mary wants others to believe that she is a true professional. Complimenting her on an accomplishment and then gently pointing out a concern might be the better way to approach her.

Topics like room assignments, distribution of resources, and teaching assignments are public information. Whether it is Mary or any other faculty member, there is almost always a rational process for decision making, and sharing that process beforehand rather than after is important. If there is a need for an exception to the rule, or there were situations in the past that you might not be aware of, it is better to know about them before a final decision has been made.

As adult professionals, we should all be willing to take responsibility for our actions. Unless an issue is particularly sensitive and you have been asked to maintain it in confidence by a faculty or staff member, sharing concerns at faculty meetings, or in newsletters, is also a useful strategy for dealing with requests that are made of you. If appropriate, the person making the request should know that she will be asked to share it with fellow faculty so that everyone has a chance to hear it at the same time and receive the same information. When offered this opportunity, Mary decided to withdraw her request.

Ultimately, Mary has decisions to make. She can decide to appreciate your candor, or she can decide to resent you because you are challenging her and bringing her behavior out into the light. She can decide to thank you for making the extra effort to locate other opportunities for her, or she can decide to be angry because you are not giving her what she wants.

Personal Reflection

Mary has provided you with a wonderful opportunity to model problem-solving, or you can very easily allow yourself to get caught up in the drama. Those on the faculty who crave drama would love to see you react emotionally to Mary.

By choosing objectivity, you allow yourself to look at Mary and the other challenges that you know are coming your way as puzzles to be solved. Life is going to continue regardless of how you respond to any of these issues. And years from now when faculty look back on you and your leadership, they will not likely recall the content of most of the decisions you made, but they will remember your conduct in making those decisions.

A college president once shared that many of his colleagues secretly expressed how much they disliked attending public board meetings. Often, students and faculty would be present to complain about matters. Administrators would often be called names or challenged for decisions that had to be made. This would happen in front of board members and other school leaders and was often embarrassing.

However, this president decided that he was going to turn board meetings into "events." He had members of the chorus come and sing. He would have teams come and be recognized for accomplishments, individual professors would receive awards for special contributions, and support staff would be given commendations for their work.

In other words, he *decided* that board meetings would be fun and celebratory. By the same token, with Mary as one of your first challenges, you have the option of seeing her as an opportunity that can help you and the department grow or as a problem that continues to exacerbate an old wound.

NINE

Antoine: Self-Centered Aggressive Resistor

"If you are losing your soul and you know it, then you've still got a soul left to lose."

—Charles Bukowski

You have spent several years in higher education and worked at a handful of different institutions before landing in your present position. Your experience has provided you with the opportunity to observe hundreds of professors over the years and never, in all of those years, have you run into anyone quite like Antoine.

Antoine has been a social science professor in the department for nineteen years. He came to the college after having been a tenured professor at a small school in the Midwest. When he first arrived he was well received by colleagues as well as students. At that time, the highlight of each semester in his classes was when he enacted a humorous rendition of "Casey at the Bat." Antoine recited the entire passage from memory and play-acted Casey, including the running of the bases to the applause of his students.

In his eighth year, he applied for the assistant dean position but did not receive it. Four years later, with two children preparing to go off to college, he was very open about the fact that he was feeling a lot of pressure to make more money, and he opened a restaurant business with his brother-in-law.

It became obvious, very quickly, that Antoine's commitment to his profession declined as his energies toward the restaurant increased. Unfortunately, in less than a year and a half, the business closed and Antoine could often be heard blaming his brother-in-law for the failure of the enterprise.

Within a few months, Antoine's next venture involved purchasing two laundromats, and he was often seen running off during the day in order to meet repairmen, make trips to the bank, and to fill in when an attendant did not show up for work.

At this point, Antoine's performance as a professor reached an all-time low, not just for him, but compared to any other faculty member in the entire college. His student evaluations were horrendous. On an A–F scale, his average grades from students were consistently in the D–F range. Most fellow professors who had previously worked with him on projects made a point of avoiding him when opportunities arose to write grants, conduct special projects, or participate in other initiatives, because of his lack of commitment and unwillingness to carry his load.

Interestingly, a small group of peers continued to interact with Antoine and were supportive of him. This group was made up of other Resistors and a couple of Reluctants, and while they were well aware of students' complaints about him, and the perception that he was not doing his share of the work in the department, they also saw safety in numbers. Having Antoine commiserate with them in their complaining added to their own validation. He also had a great deal of persuasive ability and was able to spin efforts being made by others to portray department leadership as a threat to his cadre of friends.

On an individual level, as previous department chairs attempted to work with him to get him back to being productive, Antoine denied any problems existed. Student evaluations were dismissed as sour grapes or unrealistic expectations on the part of those enrolled in his classes and the chairs that met with him.

Concerns that he was not staying aligned with the curriculum that he was teaching and that had been adopted by the department were viewed by him as an attack on his academic freedom. Antoine considered subpar surveys of the social sciences program by graduating seniors to be the result of poor performance by another professor who also taught similar classes, even though that professor's individual teaching evaluations were consistently higher than his own.

Antoine had become Teflon Man. He went out of his way to avoid responsibility for any of the concerns that existed. And while you were aware in general terms of the situation with him, you were not aware of the extent of it until you came back into the chair position and spoke with the dean and assistant dean, and read past evaluations, emails, and letters that had been placed in his personnel file. A number of disgruntled students, peers, school supervisors, and teachers that had interacted with him had filed complaints over the years.

In addition to his work with students, Antoine was required to regularly work with principals and teachers in the schools where his students would do their fieldwork. Where he was once a welcome partner, complaints started to come to your office that Antoine was not showing up on

time for observations. In addition, when he did attend, he would typically depart before a lesson was completed. His file also included letters
from some principals saying that they would not accept student teachers
if he was assigned to their schools.

While you have witnessed professors experiencing individual difficul-
ties with a student or teacher or peer now and then, you had never seen
one individual garner such a degree of dislike and animosity from across
the spectrum of personnel involved in a program.

As you read through Antoine's file you realized that a number of
attempts had been made by previous chairs to reach out to him about
these concerns. Whether he really believed his denials were authentic or
he merely saw them as a means of deflecting and stalling the conversations, you do not know. What you are aware of is that the first of your
three guiding principles is to respond to the needs of students, and Antoine has failed to do that. Not only are students not being treated well,
they are being given little guidance and, in many instances, almost totally
ignored. For many students, opportunities to learn and grow have been
negated by his behavior.

Previous attempts to improve Anthony's performance have included
a number of conversations with department chairs. You see that two
different chairs had shown Antoine copies of letters that had been sent to
them by students, supervising teachers, and principals, and he was defensive in rationalizing his behaviors in all of those instances.

One letter in his file was from a now-retired professor who complained about Antoine's failure to write sections of a grant that they were
to co-author. She and Antoine had each been given release time from
teaching a course to write a major proposal, and in the end she had to
write and rewrite the bulk of it or the deadline for its submission would
have been missed. She notably "copied" him at the bottom of the letter,
making it clear that she was so angry that she was willing to let him
know that her letter was being submitted and that if the grant were to be
funded, she refused to work with him on it.

The bulk of your next meeting with the dean focuses on Antoine. You
let her know that you have taken some time to reflect on what you have
read and observed over the years. Having access to the personnel files
has filled in a number of gaps for you.

The dean shares her own views about much of what has occurred and
acknowledges that she has had several conversations with Human Resources about Antoine. She lets you know that HR seems to have a natural resistance to taking disciplinary action or considering a dismissal of a
tenured staff member. The cost and uncertainty make them wary of getting into such procedures, and they make it clear that they would need an
extremely convincing set of evidence before taking any action. And while
Antoine's file certainly has some depth to it, much of it is arguable and
does not present them with what they feel is a "slam-dunk" case.

As you prepare to deal with Anthony, this leaves you with a question faced by many new chairs: Do I respond to people based on their history, or do I totally ignore their past and give them a fresh start? Those who favor the former argue that previous leaders spent a lot of psychological capital dealing with faculty and staff who have had issues. It is justifiable to say that the hard work and stress that these predecessors expended should be respected, and if personnel crossed lines, they should not think that they automatically get those transgressions erased from the memory bank.

In this case, the new chair should be able to make it clear to anyone involved in past misbehavior that their history is being considered as consequences are being determined.

Another aspect to think about is that failing to consider the work that a leader puts into a difficult personnel situation encourages people in leadership roles to ignore problems, particularly when the leader is in his or her last year in the position. After all, why bother to take on a difficult problem that is likely to cause sleepless nights if the effort is only going to be ignored when a new replacement comes on board?

On the other hand, employees often respond to new supervisors differently. Someone might feel that a conflict with a prior supervisor had tainted their relationship and as a result, they were never able to clear the air with that individual and move forward in a productive manner. The perception that, "He had it out for me," or "Our beliefs are just totally different," often prevents people from being able to establish healthy and fruitful relationships. A lack of skill in communication, negotiation, and compromise keeps them from ever clearing up differences.

As a result, these relationships continue to exist without ever maximizing their potential. Distrust, lack of respect, and eventual cynicism are common manifestations that play out, and often, like a virus, spread to others.

As a result, when a new leader enters the picture, some people feel that there is an opportunity to show that the problems that existed in the past were not their fault, but rather the responsibility of the past leader. They may work hard to develop a positive relationship with the new person who has come on board as a way of validating their belief: "See, it was her fault, not mine . . ."

This path is an easier one to subscribe to because the new leader does not have to refer back to historical issues in discussions. In fact, some new leaders do not even look at personnel files at all, feeling that this allows them more complete objectivity.

Ultimately, you and the dean decide that the best way to deal with Antoine is a compromise—to have you review his history, but not use it as a basis for immediate action. You agree to give him a fresh start and see where things lead.

FIRST STEPS

Ultimately, you determine that you will approach Antoine the same way you approached Anthony. You will let him know that you look forward to working with him and providing whatever help and resources you can, so that students can be provided with an excellent education, as you work together in a civil manner to continually build the department's program.

If problems do occur, you will then employ the principles of progressive discipline. At the lowest level, if it is necessary to follow up after hearing a complaint, an initial conversation will take place. You will listen to his side of the story, and whatever facts or evidence you have will then be shared with him. If in fact it appears that a change in behavior is required, you will be clear about the expectation. If appropriate, you will offer assistance if he needs help in following through on what is being asked of him.

If Antoine seems agreeable and willing to make adjustments, you may decide to end the conversation at this point. If he appears to be insincere or defensive, you may need to write a note to him reiterating what was agreed upon.

At the next level, if Antoine continues to behave in ways that are contrary to expectations, another conversation will take place. Once again, expectations will be made clear and "possible" consequences outlined if he does not meet them. This time, a follow-up letter to Antoine will be sent with a copy to the dean and to his personnel folder (this may vary slightly depending on the state and the bargaining agreement).

Continuing disregard may result in more stringent measures. The dean will likely have you call Human Resources to make sure you are following proper protocol, but next steps might include a fine or suspension depending on your local procedures. Ultimately, dismissal may occur if the problem continues through the first three levels and Antoine continues to refuse to meet institutional requirements.

This determination will be made at levels above your role as department chair and will likely include the dean, HR personnel, and possibly even the provost or president, depending on factors such as the seriousness of his infractions.

However, and as the dean has pointed out to you in previous conversations, the university will work hard to be consistent in the treatment of personnel who have violated rules. Because of this, it is important to keep in communication with HR throughout your dealings with Antoine to make sure that you handle any actions involving him in an appropriate manner.

SCHOOL STARTS

The first week of school is spent making sure that there are adequate chairs in each classroom, technology glitches are fixed, rosters are cleaned up, and freshmen are given help in locating their classrooms.

On the second day of classes, four young women come to the office together to ask if they can be transferred out of Antoine's class to another. When you ask why, they say they had him in the past and did not want to be in his room again. With further questioning, they share that he was a half hour late for the first class, a pattern that was common in their past experience, and they anticipated that the outcomes for this class would be much the same as last year's—that they would get virtually no feedback on their work nor help that would allow them to develop their skills as new professionals.

One of the women also mentions that her dad is vice president at the neighboring community college and is very concerned about this and will be calling you later today.

You realize that the time has come to address Antoine's performance. The students who came to visit you were specific about the concerns they raised, and you need to make sure you understand the whole picture. You know that specific information will be helpful when you meet with Antoine on this matter, and so you ask them if they can give you any evidence to back up their complaints.

They came well prepared, and each of them pulled out several papers that they had handed in during the previous semester. The young woman whose father was the community college administrator had apparently "coached" them on the kind of data they needed to present to you. Altogether, they give you over twenty papers and each of them, on the last page, has a "Happy Face" with a smile on it. Period. No comments, no suggestions, no evidence that the papers were ever read.

They also tell you that if you want a sworn statement saying that he was regularly late for classes in the past, as well as the first class of this year, they would be glad to give it to you, but they want assurance they will be transferred out before doing so.

One piece of advice you were given years before was to never make an important decision without first giving yourself time to think, if possible. You thank the students and tell them that their concerns will be addressed. You let them know that their educational experience is your primary concern. You also tell them that a mass exodus from a class, which could occur if you allow them to move out, would be very problematic since there is not another section available that has room for them. You ask that they give you twenty-four hours to think about this and promise to get back to them. You also assure them that your conversation will be kept in strict confidence and they have nothing to fear.

Conversations such as these are common in virtually every college department office. Whether justified or not, there will always be instances of students that find faults with professors and feel discriminated against or disliked. In the vast majority of cases, chairs have discussions with professors and typically clarify the background to these concerns: students who believe they should have had higher course grades, students who fail to submit all assignments or turn them in later than outlined by the syllabus, work that was handed in that did not respond to the assignment given or was subpar, and other performance-related deficiencies such as low test evaluations.

Most professors keep good notes, and veterans have even learned to make copies of papers or tests when they perceive a "red flag" and intuitively sense that a follow-up complaint may occur. However, the complaints against Antoine are in line with the concerns that were outlined in his personnel file. You immediately recall your agreement with the dean to read the file but hold it in abeyance any judgements in order to give Antoine a fresh start. It now seems that was a wise decision.

Obviously, your message to faculty that this semester should be seen as a new beginning was not fully digested by everyone, at least not by Antoine. You will find out if there are others as the semester continues. In the meantime, you consider all you have heard, go back and review his file once more, and on your drive home that evening give the dean a call. When she asks you with a cheery voice how the first week is going, you share that things have been quite busy and that an issue with Antoine has come up today that you would like to talk about.

"Already?" she asks.

"Yup," you respond.

She asks you to tell her about it, and so you do. After hearing what you learned, she asks what you think.

"Even though we hoped for the best, I guess that there is a certain reality here that I figured was likely to show up. I really don't think there is any choice. I have to meet with him, share the information, and unless I hear something I am not expecting, let him know very directly what is expected. It has to be stopped now."

The dean agrees. "You're right. If you let it go on it will only get worse. I know this is your first time meeting with him, but his history of behavior is a little more serious than most. I would suggest you make sure you follow up your meeting with a letter. See how he responds: If you think he gets it, don't put anything in his personnel file, but if he is argumentative, feel free to copy me and his file. Also, if you think he might not be willing to cooperate, I'm here. You can tell him to make an appointment with me."

The dean shares one other concern: "Be sure that these students are totally protected. They absolutely are not to take any heat from him. It would be best if he doesn't know who complained, obviously. Let him

know that any actions against students would have serious consequences."

THE MEETING

You want to be fair with Antoine, but you also want to be sure to protect
the students who complained. In notifying him that you need to meet,
you have decided that it is best to simply say that some concerns have
arisen and you would like to meet with him, and ask him to provide
some times either prior to or after one of his classes so you can get
together.

When the time comes, Antoine enters your office, and you behave
formally, greeting him and standing and shaking his hand. You invite
him to take a seat, look directly at him, and share the concerns that have
arisen:

> You: *Antoine, I have had some students come to me with concerns about your
> class.*

> Antoine: *Well, that's not uncommon. Kids are always complaining about
> professors. I'm sure that students complained about you at times too.*

Antoine is aware that the discussion is going to be uncomfortable and
wants to shift the discussion away from him. Acknowledging his comment but keeping on track is important.

> You: *No doubt. But these were pretty specific concerns about you, and I'd like
> to focus on them right now. For instance, they claimed that the very first night
> of class you were a half hour late getting there.*

> Antoine: *I may have been a few minutes late, but . . .*

> You: *Ok, well we both know that can happen at times, but it's important that
> you minimize it. It would be good if you made sure you provided yourself with
> plenty of time to get to class. Is there anything I can do to help you make that
> happen or can you handle it?*

Asking an adult if he needs help getting to class on time makes you want
to shake your head in wonder but you will have to hold that in until later.
At this point, whether he was thirty minutes or fifteen minutes late is not
the issue. You want to show your concern and project yourself as professionally as possible.

The problem here is his tardiness, and it needs to stop. There will be
other points in this conversation that will likely require more energy, and
you do not want to give equal weight to every infraction since some are
more important than others. The bottom line is, he knows you are aware
that he has been late. He now knows what you expect, and you have
offered help if he needs it.

Antoine concurs that he understands the need to be on time and says that he does not require any special assistance to make that happen in the future. Amen, and with that issue taken care of, you move on to your next concern, his failure to provide feedback and direction.

> You: *The other concern that has come to me is a perception that you have failed to provide students with feedback on the work they hand in.*

Here you are careful to use the word "perception." Antoine may have evidence that you do not know about that would contradict what you are saying. It is doubtful, but you have only heard one side of the story from the students.

You are also purposeful in saying ". . . failed to provide students with feedback" because you want to hear what he has to say before going into more specifics. Does he consider his smiley faces feedback? Did he give actual feedback on most assignments, but the students who came to see you only selected papers in which he had not commented? It is always important to get both sides of the story before making any charges.

> Antoine: *Well that's not true. I always acknowledge the work students do and get their papers back to them. Who is this coming from, anyway?*
>
> You: *When you say "acknowledge," what do you mean? Do you put comments on every paper?*

At this point you are not even responding to his question of "who" complained. If he pushes it, you will simply tell him that you cannot share that information since the students felt concerned about having their names made public.

> Antoine: *Well, if I have time. But they definitely know that I have reviewed them.*
>
> You: *How do they know that?*

You want an answer to this. It would be easy to answer the question for him, but don't. Let him tell you that it is his smiley faces.

> Antoine: *I kind of mark them off.*

Notice, he does not answer the question directly, nor does he elaborate further. So now you have to ask.

> You: *You mean with smiley faces?*
>
> Antoine: *Well, yeah. They see that I took the time to review them, because they see that mark at the end of the paper.*
>
> You: *So Antoine, does the smiley face mean Satisfactory or Unsatisfactory? Does it represent an "A" paper? Or "B" or "C," or what? And if there are no comments or other direction, how do they get better as writers or improve in the skill or knowledge that you are focusing on?*

Now you are getting to the seriousness of the matter. It has been hard to talk about smiley faces as a standard response to student work in a university environment. Try to picture being in a hearing or in court, or reading a newspaper article and seeing a professor defend that.

Antoine knows he looks less than professional at this point. But he is also cornered. The standard response for a cornered academic is the following . . .

> Antoine: *I think you are talking about academic freedom here. I have a right to grade and evaluate the students as I see fit.*

While you anticipate this response, nonetheless, you stare at him for a pregnant pause. Not for dramatic effect, but because you really, truly cannot believe that the person sitting across from you, who holds a PhD, is saying this. And once again, you must keep your cool, speak in an even tone, and respond professionally.

> You: *Antoine, I don't know that we agree on that point. I believe we have a responsibility, ethically, and possibly legally, to provide more than happy faces on papers. It would be great if you would put comments on the papers that give students direction both on their writing and on how they could improve. Are you OK with that?*

At this point you are hopeful that Antoine will agree to read and respond to papers, as well as get to class on time. If he does not appear to be willing to cooperate, you have the option to (calmly) let him know that it will be necessary for him to meet with you and the dean to determine where you will go next.

Assuming he does agree, however grudgingly, it is important that the conversation end on a very clear note.

> You: *Antoine, I appreciate your agreeing to go along with what we have discussed today in terms of next steps. We have both been here a long time, and I know that you are capable of being an effective professor. If there is anything that I can do that will help you, all you have to do is ask.*
>
> *I also want you to understand that I have reviewed your personnel file and when I heard the concerns raised by the students who came to the office, I found that their comments were very similar to complaints that have been made about you over the last few years. I looked at your evaluations, and they are the poorest in the department. There are letters and notes based on phone calls made to previous chairs that echo the comments of others.*
>
> *You are too talented to do this. If the kinds of complaints that I have received were to continue, I want you to understand that I will take steps to follow up on this concern that may result in disciplinary action. Am I clear?*

You should only rarely say that "disciplinary action WILL occur." If someone behaves in an inappropriate manner, such as being late for work, but then resolves the problem for a lengthy period of time, it is unlikely you are going to discipline them for being late one day, months later. Using the phrase "disciplinary action *may* occur" provides more latitude.

While difficult, this conclusion is critical. Behaviors like those that Antoine and a handful of other members of the department are manifesting have to stop. You understood that conceptually when you took the job; now you are facing it operationally.

There is also a good chance that what you are doing is going to be known by other members of the department, shortly. While it is imperative that you, as chair, do not share this conversation with anyone other than the dean, you cannot control Antoine.

You should expect that Antoine will let his support group know that you have called him in and likewise, you know full well that he is going to paint a picture of being victimized by you. You cannot control that, but you can control what you do with him and how you behave toward others. And in reality, in most of these situations the peer group knows the real truth but lacks the integrity and courage to tell their colleague to clean up his act.

Further, while your first priority is to make sure that Antoine treats students with respect, it is completely legitimate for you to send a message to all faculty that there are certain standards you will observe that are nonnegotiable, particularly in relation to the three guiding principles you have repeatedly stated.

Just how the Antoine in this story responded, or the Antoines on other faculties will respond, will vary based on a number of factors: what they believe they can get away with, resentment level, degree of job security, anger quotient, and all the other various factors that are involved in complex human dynamics.

All leaders have a certain amount of legislated authority within which they can work. An approach like the one described here allows a faculty member the chance to be effective and successful without painful intrusion into their lives. It really is quite simple. Come to class on time, follow the syllabus, provide good instruction, give students feedback, and grade them fairly. It's done by hundreds of thousands of teachers every day.

Some will take the opportunity given to them, and some will choose not to. School leaders can only play the cards they have been dealt. In this case, if Antoine chooses to continue his aberrant behaviors, escalating his case to the dean is the obvious next step.

What chairs should know before getting deeply involved in a problem with a faculty member is where the dean is likely to fall if problems do continue to occur. No superior can be asked to make commitments ahead of time because circumstances and details change. However, a general understanding and sense of what the chair, dean, provost, and president stand for is critical. An old saying provides good advice: "Don't engage in a battle you don't have a reasonably good chance of winning." If this occurs, you are best advised to return to faculty ranks or sharpen your resume and look for another position.

OTHER THOUGHTS AND ADVICE
ON DEALING WITH RESISTORS

If one were to point to a single group of people who have the most negative impact on a faculty as well as on school leaders, it is the Resistors. Antoine is not a real person but a composite of a number of individuals that have been observed over several years in school leadership.

There is no one answer to how to respond to Antoine and other Resistors. Each has to be responded to on a case-by-case basis. However, there are some things we have learned that can often be applied across a number of these different situations.

First, deal with matters immediately. Allowing them to continue will likely result in the problems getting bigger and more difficult. It also sends a message to others that an ignored transgression is an acceptable transgression to leadership if it is allowed to perpetuate.

Second, transparency is almost always an advantage. Most leaders we have met do not have an interest in cultivating conflicts and making their lives or the lives of their faculty and staff more difficult. When all of the facts are on the table, people are more likely to understand why certain decisions are made.

Also realize that as a leader you are not always able to put all facts on the table. Certain areas, such as personnel matters or issues that may end up in a court or other kind of hearing, may have to be kept confidential. While this may not always be preferred, people in professional settings understand it.

Third, as noted previously, people in university leadership are probably the most poorly prepared of any group in a professional organization. Lacking any kind of required training or experience to take a position, they often have no understanding of how contracts and unions intersect with their daily responsibilities. Since many chairs are or were union members, they should use that experience to build a relationship with the union and consider them allies rather than adversaries.

Some people might have difficulty accepting this idea, but the reality is that most union representatives want the same things that school leaders want—effective instructors serving students. Just like defense attorneys, union representatives are required to advocate for faculty members. However, good union reps know when someone is working within guidelines and when they are not.

As a chair or dean you will never hear them tell you that their client was wrong and should be disciplined (well, maybe after they retire and you talk about the good old days they might). However, most of the people in rep positions are smart and very experienced. If someone they represent is out of line, they will pull them aside and privately let them know that they need to make changes or they are likely to get into trouble.

Once a relationship of trust is established with a union rep, a lot of potential problems can be avoided through cooperative, preemptory conversations. However, be sensitive to the fact that trust in this relationship is critical. Once trust with a union rep (or vice versa) is broken, it will most likely never be reestablished.

A fourth recommendation for dealing with Resistors is to find creative ways of problem solving. There are a lot of parallels between dealing with problematic university faculty and problematic K–12 faculty. Both have very strong unions (in fact the unions representing both groups are the same in many instances) and consequently have similar types of job protections.

Over the years, K–12 leaders have exercised strategies to support and redirect behaviors that university leaders should learn from. For instance, teachers who are not effective in the classroom are often provided professional development. In such instances, an individual teacher might be asked to spend time with another faculty member with a strong reputation. This might be someone in another district or someone from within the university itself, depending on what is most appropriate.

One teacher might also be asked to team-teach with another highly effective teacher and be given specific things to observe and look for. In these cases, periodic meetings with the chair should take place to assure the process is occurring as expected. And chairs should note: that this type of recommendation should not just be considered for individuals who are problematic, but also any members of a department who are looking to refresh or develop their skills.

Shadowing is another useful tool. This might be done in cases where supervision takes place. In all of these instances, a cooperative triad including the teacher, the "mentor" teacher, and the university chair will be most effective. Cooperatively setting goals up front and sharing them within the triad is important, along with the aforementioned meetings as a way to keep track of progress and discuss what is seen.

Observing exemplary model teachers is always a useful tool. Many public schools have adopted formative assessment models in which teams of teachers observe and provide feedback to each other to enhance student learning. This is not part of an instructor's official file but is strictly used as a tool for growth.

On an individual level, one school had an instructor observe a teacher in another university. In this case doing so was less threatening for the instructor who was visiting.

Another option that has been used with some success is "counseling out." Antoine's heart is no longer in his work. After years of doing the same thing, he is not passionate about coming to work and teaching and advising students any longer. Remuneration for his efforts will never be at a level that he would like to achieve.

A third party who might be able to help Antoine establish his business interests might be considered. Locating someone from the business college in the university that works in the area of small business development might be of interest to Antoine. This individual would not have any involvement in the problems that exist with Antoine's work in the department. She would strictly be an advisor and counselor in the area of business development.

Related to this, the dean could provide assistance by making a leave of absence available to Antoine for a year. This would give him a chance to see if in fact the grass is greener. If he has success and finds greater happiness outside of the university, it works to everyone's advantage.

EXPLANATION OF ANTOINE'S BEHAVIORS

At this point, Antoine's behaviors primarily fall in the Passive-Aggressive and Aggressive categories of the Axis of Negative Behaviors. His passive behaviors tend to highlight his resistance. He is often late to classes, cuts his supervision short when visiting students in the field, and does not meet deadlines or show up regularly to meetings. More aggressively, he orchestrates dissent with his fellow Resistors when opportunities arise and can be hostile toward those in leadership positions when questioned about his work.

Unfortunately, opportunities to start fresh have been ignored. Antoine has no real interest in being an effective faculty member, and his priorities are making money and contributing as little as possible to the academy. Even when specific evidence shows that he is failing to support students, he does not care. As one faculty member remarked to you: "If he worked as hard at doing good work as he does avoiding it, his life would be a lot easier!"

In terms of his own psychological needs, Antoine obviously does not find his work to be fun or enjoyable. His efforts to avoid making meaningful contributions make this pretty clear. It is also obvious that Antoine is more interested in meeting his needs for fulfillment and power from areas outside of education. For him, developing a successful business and making money appear to be more important than positive evaluations from students or the respect of peers.

As far as affiliation and belonging, Antoine has chosen to get this from his fellow Resistors. Appreciation from students, other peers in the department, and school leadership are secondary to his power needs. As a result, he has been willing to forego the latter for the former.

MORE EFFECTIVE MEANS TO ENGAGE ANTOINE

Antoine requires careful handling. His past behaviors cannot be totally dismissed simply because you are a new chair. At the same time, you want to make every effort to allow him the opportunity to be an effective and contributing member of the department. As a result, engaging with him early on and letting him know your intention to be supportive of him as a professional is important.

If several of the suggestions described above are tried and unsuccessful, or if Antoine refuses to take any assistance, you have little choice but to follow the next steps in progressive discipline. If Antoine takes actions that continue to violate the expectations that have been laid out for him, you need to call him in. If the discussion verifies this continued defiance, you and the dean need to speak with Human Resources about potential next steps. These might include a reprimand, suspension, a fine, or even charges for dismissal.

Personal Reflection

While meeting the expectations of your dean and provost is important to you, there really is a higher authority that you have to answer to . . . your own conscience. Leadership often calls for compromises. Anyone who wants to go into a chair or dean's or other administrative position at a university must reconcile the fact that there are times that they will be called upon to make or accept decisions that they do not agree with. However, anyone taking one of those positions must also have a moral compass that identifies their ultimate boundaries.

The idea of enabling someone like Antoine is more than some chairs can handle. If you have determined that he is truly providing a bad educational experience for students, and in some cases is demeaning some individuals, then you have to also decide how far you will go to assure those behaviors are stopped and stricter actions are taken against him.

Ultimately, after looking carefully at all of the facts, you have to look in the mirror and determine whether you and your conscience can accept your own responses.

These cases are among the most difficult for people in leadership. As noted at the start of this book, people in education enter the profession because they enjoy working with others. Having to deal with discipline and conflict is hard. At the same time, school leaders have to remember their first responsibility—the care and support of the students in their institutions. The only thing worse than a professor treating students poorly is a school leader allowing it to continue.

TEN

Sandy: Committed Reluctant and Wanda: Junior-Level Committed

"The real voyage of discovery consists not in seeking new landscapes, but in seeing with new eyes."

—Marcel Proust

As you have begun to work through some of the personnel challenges brought on by faculty and staff, you realize that your initial conversation with the designated people in categories such as Committed, Reluctant, and Resistors was not quite as clean and clear as you had originally anticipated.

In fact, no one really falls into just one category, but rather they move across and up and down within categories depending on situations, personalities, timing, and various other factors that may exist at a given moment. Certainly, based on the strength of their behaviors, some people fall primarily under one label or another, but you have come to realize that everyone, including yourself, the dean, and others that you have interacted with over the years, is open to change at a given moment.

Sandy is an excellent example of a faculty member who spans the scale from Committed to Reluctant to Resistor depending on the situation and the people that surround him. Overall, when you consider his commitment to students and work ethic, you do not believe in your heart that he is a Reluctant. He exhibits a Committed persona when serving students and is more of a Resistor when he is around Anthony and some of the other Resistors.

It appears he has never been comfortable within any one category. As a fourteen-year tenured faculty member, Sandy is well thought of by his students. Last year, he was recognized as Professor of the Year at graduation. This award is based on a vote by students and considered a real honor in the college.

While dedicated, Sandy is an anomaly. As popular as he is with students, he has put a wall between himself and many of the faculty in the department. He is possibly Anthony's biggest advocate. While you have never heard him praise Anthony or talk about his contributions to the college or students, he regularly has coffee with him and they are often seen having lunch together.

When Anthony has engaged in behaviors that try to undermine efforts by administration, Sandy has consistently, and quietly, been by his side. You are aware that Anthony and Sandy's spouses are close friends and have assumed over the years that this has something to do with Sandy's loyalty to Anthony.

Since Sandy has remained relatively passive about becoming engaged in problems involving Anthony, you have not had any cause to be concerned about him. However, that situation recently changed after you received a visit from Wanda, another member of the social science faculty who has been with the department for two years.

Wanda: *Thanks for seeing me. I wanted to talk to you about something that has come up. As you know, I've worked with Sandy over the last school year and much of the summer on the federal grant we submitted to train teachers in using DBQs, document-based questions.*

You: *Of course, that was a great accomplishment. I had a chance to read the proposal during the summer, and it sounds really exciting. Congratulations.*

Wanda: *Thanks, but something has occurred that we need to talk about. We put some money in the budget for faculty to work with Sandy and me in the training. I just discovered that Sandy has earmarked a good chunk of the money for Anthony's involvement as a trainer. This just won't work. You know how he is. Students complain about him; he doesn't prepare. If he is involved I'm afraid that things won't go well and we'll get poor evaluations from the participants. If that happens, our chances of any further funding go down the drain. Plus it will kill our reputation out in the community. Geez. Think about him in faculty meetings—he falls asleep half the time. This would be a disaster.*

You: *I understand your concerns. You don't feel comfortable talking with Sandy about it?*

Wanda: *Quite honestly, Sandy and I shared the work on the grant and we are co-directors, but he's been here for years and I'm still the newbie. I'm not comfortable telling him he can't involve Anthony. I don't know what to do.*

You: *Well, tell me what you want.*

Wanda: *Quite simply, I don't want Anthony involved in the grant. This is a big deal for me. A successful project could be a huge plus when I go up for tenure. It also would be a factor in any continued funding. On the other hand, a project that receives poor evaluations is going to reflect badly on me as well as the college.*

Honestly, I don't see any compromises that can be made with this. If he's up in front of teachers who are giving their time to do this it will be a disaster. And we don't have fluff money in the grant to pay him for some kinds of menial work.

You: *Okay, Wanda. I hear you. Let me think about this and see if we can come up with a strategy for addressing it.*

The conversation concerns you. For one thing, you have always found that you could figure out creative answers to most problems. But in this situation, there does not seem to be a lot of room for creativity. After some thought, it occurs to you that two heads are better than one and perhaps you should talk with the dean to explore other possibilities.

You: *I assume you read my note outlining what's going on with Wanda and Sandy and the grant?*

Dean: *Yes, thanks for the summary. So what are your thoughts? Have you come up with any plans for handling it?*

You: *I really don't know how to address this one without causing some conflict. I wanted to talk with you and see if between the two of us we might be able to come up with some ideas.*

Dean: *Well, first of all, I did look at the grant budget, which I had to sign. If your goal is to try to give Anthony money for some kind of service to the grant, that would be tough to do. Other than stipends for the directors and materials and supplies, and the dollars for doing training, the remainder of the money is all to be used for payments to the teachers undergoing staff development.*

You: *Would you want to provide a stipend out of college funds for some services to the project? He could help with developing materials, organizing meetings, and so on.*

Dean: *You don't say that with a great deal of enthusiasm.*

You: *You're right, I don't. Everything Wanda said was accurate. As you know, he and Sandy are tight, and I'm sure that's why Sandy put him in the grant. But he really should have gotten approval from me before he made any financial commitments.*

Dean: *This is true. So think about what you've just said. First, Anthony is not likely to do a satisfactory job. I will tell you now that my office will not provide any extra dollars for him. Finally, Sandy made this decision without getting approval from his co-director or his chair.*

You: *So you're telling me I should just deny his involvement in the project?*

The dean looks you in the eye and nods.

Dean: *Go back to our guiding principles. Putting Anthony in this grant is not going to help us build our program if we lose the funding or he makes us look bad. Also, neither you nor I owe Anthony anything. This is work that goes above and beyond the contract. He has no right to it. Do you really want to publicly reward someone who has little credibility in the university?*

You and I both share the tendency to want to keep everyone happy and not cause waves unnecessarily. However, we have also talked about our commitment to do the right thing. Putting Anthony in front of these people is clearly not the right thing. Sometimes you cannot make everyone happy. However, you can at least do the right thing.

As you leave, you think about what she said. It makes sense. Send a message that rewards and recognition must be earned and not simply given. With that in mind, you call Sandy and Wanda into the office to break the news. Prior to this conversation, you have let Wanda know that it will be a follow-up to the previous conversation that took place between the two of you.

You: *Sandy, Wanda, thanks for coming in. I wanted to talk with you about the grant that you both wrote. The dean's office sent me a copy with a reminder that I should be reviewing it with you and that I need to sign off on the time, place, personnel, etc. I think it's a great program and something that is sorely needed by the area we serve. Congratulations to both of you.*

I do have one concern and that is with Anthony's inclusion in the program. I am not comfortable with his involvement. I have seen both of you present this material, and you are both absolutely great. I would much rather the two of you do the presenting.

Sandy: *Gee, I've already spoken with Anthony about this. I don't get it. What's the problem?*

You: *The issue is that the folks who participate deserve the best we have. That's you and Wanda. If you want to consider an additional faculty member, you can get back to me, but it will need to be someone with excellent presentation skills and experience in the area. If you want to invite Anthony to sit in and learn the program and develop his skills for possible future participation, I'd be glad to talk with you about that. We won't be able to pay him to do this out of the project, but he is certainly welcome to take the opportunity to learn and grow.*

Sandy: *Well, this is a little awkward because I've already talked to him about being involved.*

You: *As you know, you are supposed to clear this with the chair before making any financial commitments. Have either of you made any other offers to people other than Anthony?*

You are curious to see if Sandy makes it clear that Wanda had no involvement in this decision. He doesn't. Also, do not be too specific about why you are not allowing Anthony to be part of the project. Once again, you need to think ahead, and you do not want to say anything that could be used against you if Anthony believes you have slandered him.

Wanda: *No, not on my part.*

Sandy: *No, there weren't any others.*

You: *First of all, I really am pleased with all the hard work you put in on this. However, it would be good if you'd touch base with me in the future before making any financial commitments. At this point, it is best that one of you let Anthony know about this.*

You have been careful to keep Wanda out of this as best you can. Sandy is not happy about the decision; however, you get the impression that he is relieved to have Anthony out of the picture and doubly relieved that it was you who did it rather than him. You also know that Sandy never acknowledged the fact that he made the decision to include Anthony on his own. Does he feel some responsibility for not involving Wanda in the decision now that you have brought the matter into the open? Probably, but whether he does or not, hopefully he received the message not to do it again in the future.

EXPLANATION OF SANDY'S BEHAVIORS

Being appointed chair from the inside brings benefits as well as challenges. In a case like this one, you have known Sandy for a long time. If you used your best barometer to evaluate Sandy, you would be the first to agree that you would have your own children take his class if they attended your program. He is a great teacher and likes students, but you have never been able to figure out this blind loyalty to Anthony. Regardless of the reason, you cannot control it—you only have control over the decisions that you can make.

While the family relationship that exists may have a lot to do with their friendship, Sandy's reputation as an effective instructor and his concern for his students are diametrically opposed to Anthony's. Your guiding principles state that good education and civility are priorities. With that in mind, your best option is to accept what you have.

There are things he does well and you need to appreciate them. The fact that he supports Anthony is not typically a significant problem for you or the department. A slip like the one that has just occurred is problematic, but minor.

MORE EFFECTIVE MEANS TO ENGAGE SANDY

Depending on how well you know Sandy, you have to gauge how honest you can be when talking to him about Anthony. One good piece of advice you received long ago is to never, ever talk about one faculty member with another faculty member. No matter how well you think you know them, in the end you are management and they are faculty, and the time may come (negotiations or a grievance or other calamity) when all parties are called on to take a side.

In addition, friendships can be fragile. Somewhere along the line you may have to make a decision that angers a longtime "friend," and suddenly you may find that person is not your friend any longer.

If you are in a position of leadership, you cannot afford to be quoted by others about something that happened in the past. In this case, Sandy is fully aware of Anthony's reputation, and in reality he probably did not want Anthony in the program, but did not know how to keep him out. Your decision is actually a divine intervention for him. Even your slight rebuke about not making commitments without your approval is helpful because it takes him off the hook.

Your decision allowed Sandy to maintain his need for affiliation with Anthony. You are the bad guy; he was the friend who stood up for him. He was willing to sacrifice some power for this since it was obvious to you that he went behind Wanda's back in making the decision without your approval.

And while Sandy is a valued member of the faculty, he will make bad decisions at times just like we all do. When those instances arise, Sandy has to take responsibility for poor choices. In the big picture, what happened here is not serious or fatal. In fact, it may be a good learning experience, not just for Sandy but for you as well as the chair and the rest of the faculty when they become aware of what occurred. You have made it clear that you are keeping up with activities that take place in the department, and when it comes to your responsibilities, such as signing off on a grant, you take them seriously.

Finally, a very important lesson to be learned is that sometimes the answer is "no." This is hard for some people to accept, and in reality most effective leaders can find ways around obstacles if they are really committed to doing so. However, Anthony has not earned that consideration. He should not be carried by the system merely because he has been there a long time. Tenure protection covers him in his job; it does not cover him in duties outside of his position.

WANDA

With several characters involved in this situation, there are a number of different needs being addressed in one way or another. Wanda was the first to come to you. Because of her place in the department as a new faculty member, you see Wanda as a Junior-Level Committed at this point. She is proactive and progressive. She has identified a problem and wants to solve it. She has the potential to be a great asset to the department over time.

Wanda is the least senior Committed on the faculty, and this is a result of her personal strength. She has no fear of dealing with issues in a strong but diplomatic matter. She could have confronted Sandy but knew that it might have been counterproductive. When she considered what she wanted (getting Anthony out of the program), she was self-aware enough to know that the chair would be better able to make that happen than she would be.

After the entire process played out, Wanda got her wish. This made her feel empowered about being able to work through the system in order to resolve a problem. She also built some trust with her chair and was not put in an awkward position with Sandy. In fact, because of the way that it was handled, Sandy saw that she needed to be given greater involvement in decisions.

There are times when power can be shared and grow without boundaries when people work collegially. This is not one of those times. On the Axis of Negative Behaviors, Sandy had intended to get his way through Passive means.

He personally made a decision to have Anthony involved. At the time, he figured Wanda was a new faculty member and was not going to question him. Further, with the changeover in the chair's office taking place, it was unlikely that someone with his seniority would be questioned about his hiring of Anthony. However, this all backfired when Wanda became aware of what happened and the grant budget was brought to you for your approval.

In the end, Sandy picked up on the fact that he could not freewheel decisions related to the program. In fact, not only was he expected to communicate with the chair, but he needed to communicate with his co-director. Fortunately for him, you did not embarrass him by questioning Wanda's involvement in the Anthony decision more deeply when meeting with him and Wanda. Ultimately, you felt the message got across.

Personal Reflection

This was a learning experience for you. The conversation with the dean gives you a different perspective about problem solving. You learned that sometimes the best answer is to say "no." By establishing boundaries, everyone involved learned what is allowable and what is not. This goes beyond the three guiding principles and is a valuable part of everyday functioning.

Anthony is going to learn that he will need to earn respect and consideration. He may choose not to, but that is a decision he has to make. Sandy and others will clearly see that you are not afraid to take on tough decisions, and those decisions are based on certain principles and beliefs.

As situations like this occur, you will cross paths with virtually every member of the department at some point. With time and consistency, people will see that they can talk to someone in leadership, and if there is a reason to follow up on a concern, they know that it will happen.

ELEVEN

Andrew: Committed Reluctant and Bruce: Passive-Aggressive Resistor

"The way a team plays as a whole determines its success. You may have the greatest bunch of individual stars in the world, but if they don't play together, the club won't be worth a dime."

— Babe Ruth

Departments typically consist of a cross section of individuals who come to the workplace with varying degrees of skill, knowledge, and commitment. One of the most important things you do as a department chair is make wise choices in the hiring process. Over a period of years, colleges often change their offerings and new knowledge and abilities are needed.

You cannot help but recall one college you worked in where a dance program that once had been extremely popular failed to draw student enrollment over a period of years. Every reasonable effort was made to attract new students to the program, but interest had faded.

The dean and provost saw this trend occurring and worked with the department chair and faculty to allow instructional staff to cross-train into other areas of the college. This meant totally new assignments for some of the faculty, but these were bright, committed individuals who were devoted to the institution. They did not want to uproot their families and have to start over again as less senior professors in new institutions.

While not as profound, many universities have implemented online courses for students who are unable to attend classes on-site. Skill in operating the technology used in distance learning programs was foreign to many veteran college faculty. When first initiating these programs, most schools provided extensive staff training in how to use the new technologies in order to allow faculty to update their skill sets.

Whether a change is major, such as eliminating a department that has gone out of business, or relatively minor, such as providing training to use technology to teach courses, the institution has a responsibility to take care of its personnel, so long as students' needs continue to be met. This is reasonable, assumed, and understood by those in the institution. A comparable commitment by faculty and staff should also be expected.

Most staff members you have worked with in universities are highly motivated and concerned with doing the best job possible in service to students and their institutions. You have witnessed "senior citizen professors" reenacting Shakespeare in costume and physical education instructors demonstrating routines in gymnastics. You have seen long-term, tenured professors who are still curious about their disciplines continuing to research and write and speak with others in order to extend their understanding of their subject matter, when they could just as easily be sitting on a beach or playing or traveling. This is not the exception, but rather the rule with the majority of those with whom you have come in contact.

Unfortunately, it is also this group of faculty that may suffer most when a department becomes dysfunctional. When those who wish to talk with colleagues about building programs find themselves unable to do so because others are unwilling to come into the same room with other department members present, they feel stymied and frustrated. Even if meetings do occur, they find themselves sitting by, nervously wondering who is going to exhibit aggressive behavior and possibly make accusations or name call.

Working in such environments is frustrating. Good professionals inherently want to do things that are productive. They want to move forward and progress. When they hit a brick wall and have nowhere else to turn, they throw up their hands. Over time, feeling repressed and unable to move forward, this group of faculty becomes resentful: "Why do my colleagues act like such jerks? Why can't we deal with issues and not personalities? Why doesn't the administration fire them?" These are all common questions that productive and positive faculty members have when their peers act out or shut down.

The role of leadership in dealing with this group is to provide them support, hope, and assurance. Support needs to be both psychological and tangible. These faculty need to realize that their efforts at being effective educators will not be hindered by a handful of recalcitrant colleagues. Whether they are in highly vulnerable positions as new professors working on being retained and promoted, or long-term veterans, they need to know that you recognize the dynamics of the environment and will protect them from being harmed by it.

These faculty members also need to feel optimistic that hope for the future is realistic and reachable. The role of leadership in this environment is crucial. A leader who acts beaten and hopeless is very likely to project that mood onto those around him. As a chair you need to constantly emphasize the positive, recognize those who have accomplished important goals or activities, and model optimism for others. In addition to emphasizing the positive, it is important to minimize the negative. Do not allow the "mountain out of a molehill" phenomenon to occur.

It is not uncommon to have a person or two who relishes the opportunity to point out a failure, problem, gap, or misstep. In reality, we all experience these mistakes regularly. What is important is to avoid drowning in them. It is rare that anything occurs that is fatal to a reputation or livelihood. Everyone makes errors and we have a choice in how we view those errors. They can be viewed as problems or as opportunities from which to learn and grow.

Assurance needs to be visible and accomplished by concrete actions. Anyone old enough to be a college professor is old enough to have experiences with people who are proficient in the use of rhetoric. Too many leaders make reassuring comments: "I have an open-door policy." This sounds great. But if after listening to a concern nothing happens, the open door might just as well have stayed shut. Or, "We are like a family here," until someone makes a mistake and is then disenfranchised from the so-called family without first being given reasonable support.

Those who are truly committed need to see substantive, meaningful action on the part of leaders. When a Committed or Reluctant witnesses a Resistor blatantly violating a norm or practice, she is going to look closely at what happens next. If leadership fails to show the courage to deal with infractions, good faculty will wear down.

Consider the following conversation that took place with Andrew, a member of the science faculty:

Andrew: *Hi, how's our new chair doing?*

You: *Great, Andrew. And you? How's your year starting out?*

Andrew: *I'm okay, but I have a concern that I need to talk to you about. As you know, I coordinate the comprehensive exam that all of our students must take in order to graduate from the program. And I also teach the Field Research II course every spring. All of our graduate students take Field Research I in the fall with Bruce or Ronald before they get to me.*

You: *Right. They outline their field research project in the fall and then they collect and report on it in the spring with you, correct?*

Andrew: *Correct. And they write the first three chapters of their thesis in the first course and then the final two chapters with me. That's where the problem comes up. We've been using this format for two years now. I couldn't help but notice last year that several of the students did poorly in my Field Research II class. We have independent readers review their papers and almost a dozen students received an Unacceptable grade on the research portion of the comprehensive examination.*

Those students whose work was evaluated as unacceptable failed to meet standard criteria in how to conduct a study. Their understanding of research questions was lacking or incomplete. Methodologies often did not align with the research, and what they considered to be examples of literature reviews did not always address the topic in a focused manner.

This meant that the students had to come back to retake the comp exam. The worst part is, they could not graduate on time plus they had to pay tuition to retake the course.

You: *Ouch. I don't have a problem with some students failing. In fact, if every student passed each time we administered it, I would wonder if we require enough rigor. But that's a pretty large percentage you are talking about.*

Andrew: *Exactly, and here's the bigger problem—I went back to the year before and found that almost the same thing happened. Further, I did an analysis and learned that all but one of the students had been in Bruce's Field Research I course the previous fall, while Ronald only had one that failed.*

You: *Wow. Since I wasn't involved in that area I wasn't aware of this. So you are saying that the students' work is evaluated through a blind review and essentially all of our failures come from Bruce's class?*

Andrew: *Yes. And while the students don't have access to that data, they are well aware of the fact that the failures are coming from Bruce's class. I have had several come to me terrified of being placed in his sections.*

You: *Damn. First of all, I appreciate your letting me know about this. I also appreciate the time you are taking with the students. I know this is not easy for you to deal with, and we need to address it. I have to do some more homework on this but before I look into it further, are there any other details that I need to know?*

It is important to allow Andrew the opportunity to share any concerns he has related to the problem. And as much as you might want to shake your head in disgust with what has happened—and you have no doubt that he is accurate in his comments about Bruce—you have to remain objective. Gathering pertinent data to verify exactly what has occurred is a necessary next step. At the same time, the semester has started and you realize that you need to move on this quickly.

Andrew: *I don't have anything further to add as far as the results we've seen, but I have to tell you, a lot of us are just tired of this. Ronald and I meet regularly to talk about the students. Bruce has been invited to join us, and he has never shown up. When I sent out a copy of the results and asked for their comments, Bruce never even responded.*

This is really discouraging. Here we are working hard at this and he doesn't seem to care. Sometimes I just want to throw up my hands.

As he continues his voice rises:

Let's be honest. You know full well that he doesn't give a damn about the students. They all know what an ass he is, and none of them want to be in his classes. He spends as little time on campus as possible, and when he is here he spends his time with Anthony and their little band of friends complaining about everybody else.

His teaching is lousy, he and his friends don't pitch in to get things done around here, and ultimately everyone else is put in the position of having to make up excuses and cover for them. I know I'm starting to sound bitter, but I'm telling you, I'm not the only one. People have had it.

Though you have just started in your position, and you know this is not something new, but a continuation of what has happened in the past, you are also aware that you must deal with this immediately. You have known Andrew for several years and you know that he is not an alarmist; in fact, he's exactly the opposite. You have observed him play the role of compromiser and peacemaker in meetings over the years. If he is this angry, it is obvious that the problems have reached a level of intensity that you cannot ignore.

The larger message is that Andrew could easily be lost if this problem is not solved in a meaningful way. He sees the inequality in Bruce's lack of effort in relation to the amount of effort that he and Ronald are providing. And further, he sees the damage that Bruce is causing students. As a conscientious professional, this is just not acceptable to him.

You: I hear you, Andrew. I need to do some homework, but I promise I will do some checking and act on what I learn. I'm asking one thing of you: Please give me a little confidence and support. I will not ignore concerns that are brought to me, but I am not in a position where I can share with you or any other faculty exactly how I am going to handle sensitive personnel matters.

I know that you are aware of the need for confidentiality in this area. However, you are going to have to trust that I will act on any concern that comes to me involving students being shortchanged or people not being treated in a civil matter. Okay?

Andrew rightfully deserves a great deal of support. He needs to know that you understand his concerns on a personal level, and he needs to actually hear you say it. Likewise, he has trusted you enough to be candid about the matter, and your assurance that you hear him and will act on what you have heard is critical. He does not need the "open door" or "we are family" message. He needs the "I hear you and I will act" message. And within a reasonable time, assuming your homework verifies all he has said. He needs to see the action take place.

This is an important point in time for you with an issue that needs to be addressed now. If you fail to take action, the chances are good that you are going to lose some trust from Andrew and possibly other members from the Committed and Reluctant groups.

Your first step is to do exactly what you told Andrew—check the data. It is imperative that you are working with accurate information. If the data provided on paper is verified, take a look at the names of students who were in Bruce's classes. There is a strong possibility that you will know some of those students, and asking them to come in and talk to you about their impressions of the total program may provide you with some additional insight.

When meeting with students you should not focus on just the Field Research and Comp courses, but ask about all of their coursework. However, when you get to the Field Research and Comp courses, listen carefully to what they have to say and be sure to ask how well prepared they felt after having taken those classes. The chances are good that the students themselves will expand on their concerns when you get to this point; however, you do not want to appear to be conducting an inquisition on a particular course or professor, since you do not want students starting rumors about your investigation.

Assuming what you learn from the paper review and meetings with students is accurate, you need to meet with Bruce and get his side of the story. While what you have at this point appears to be pretty convincing, you never know what extenuating circumstances might exist. In addition, if you do end up taking a strong action in response, it would be better to find out now how Bruce will be defending himself if you should get into a hearing or other formal action.

As always, you greet Bruce in a businesslike fashion, standing to meet his eye and shake his hand:

> You: *Bruce, thanks for coming in. I wanted to talk with you about some concerns that have come up related to the first semester Field Research course that you teach.*

> Bruce: *Oh, I didn't know there were any problems.*

> You: *It appears that we have had a number of students struggling with Field Research II and the comp exam. When I've looked at past year's results, it seems that virtually all of the students who did poorly in the research section of the exam were from your sections.*

> Bruce: *Well, I'm not sure what's going on, but a lot of the students also have Ronald, and I know that he doesn't stick to the curriculum the way it was originally laid out. I know this because I did the syllabus in the first place.*

> You: *I'm not sure if you understood me, but actually I've reviewed the work of all of the students from the past two years, and with one exception, all of the failures came from your sections.*
>
> *Here is a copy of the roster of your students who did poorly, what the problems were, and whose class they were in. Also, there are copies of their papers with yellow highlights showing the concerns. As you know, we have independent readers review these, and they did not know the students or the professors.*

> Bruce: *So is this a "beat up on Bruce" meeting?*

Data is extremely powerful. You now see that the extra time you took to review objective data was worth it. It is hard to argue with facts, and Bruce has no real justification for the results. It is also obvious from his voice and words that Bruce is feeling very defensive at this point.

> You: *I have no interest in beating up on anyone. My concern is that we take care of our students and build a strong program. What I'd like to do at this point is talk about what we can do going forward to fix the problems that exist.*

In books you have read on management science, this rational approach has resulted in the employee (Bruce in this case) seeing the error of his ways and agreeing that he will work cooperatively with the manager (you in this case) to address the problem. However, Bruce apparently has not read the same books. Bruce's voice rises as he addresses you.

> Bruce: *I think this is just a witch hunt and a lot of bunk. I'm sorry. I really thought you were the best person for this job, but apparently you are on "their side" and just want to make a scapegoat out of me. As far as I'm concerned, we are done here. I'm leaving.*

At this point, Bruce gets up and departs the office, and since you were not quite prepared for this you quickly remember a piece of wise advice you once received: "Sometimes no response is the best response." Chasing him down the hall at this moment is not likely to result in anything good happening, so you remain in your seat.

You are well aware going into this particular situation that what occurs is likely to become known to the entire department and everyone is going to be looking to see how it turns out. Andrew will undoubtedly share the fact that he saw you with his colleagues. Most likely he let them know that you promised to act on the concern. Likewise, Bruce will be meeting or on the phone with Anthony, Marianne, Mary, and other sympathizers to share his view of how he is being victimized.

As you ponder your next steps, you look up at the wall and see a poster board that brings your thoughts back into focus:

The purpose of the Secondary Education Department is to:

1. Serve our students in a responsible manner.
2. Treat all individuals we come in contact with in a civil manner.
3. Build excellent programs.

You ask yourself, "Okay, do I really mean this?" You think back to the conversations you had with the dean when you were hired, and as you look again at the statement on the wall, the next steps become very clear to you.

You write an email to Bruce and let him know that your conversation was not completed. You let him know that you would like to meet with him again before the end of the day. You also point out to him that he is welcome to bring a union representative to the meeting with him. You let him know that a copy of this email will be placed in his personnel file and another sent to the dean.

The reason for doing this is simple. If you allow Bruce to walk away, you have given him the power. You might as well hand in your own resignation from your position. It means that ultimately you have given up any authority you might have. The use of power is not something to be employed at the drop of a hat. Using it too often will only dilute it. But once in a great while you will be placed in a situation where you need to exercise your authority in a judicial, clear manner. Bruce has left you no choice but to do that.

Advising Bruce of his right to have a union representative present will surprise him. As a veteran faculty member he already knows this. However, you are the last person from whom he would be expecting to get this advice. It shows that you feel confident about what you are doing and you are not intimidated by invoking a formal process.

In addition, and something most faculty chairs never consider, think about the fact that you too are still a faculty member. You are going into this meeting and there is a good chance that Bruce will have a union representative with him. You should do the same thing. Call the union and let them know you want a representative present to sit by your side.

The dean may shake her head in wonder at this and even suggest that the assistant dean be there with you rather than a union representative. However, having a faculty representative with you provides you with a great opportunity. Your discussions with the union representative are much like those with a lawyer. You can be candid about exactly what is going on. You can share all of the information that is available (assuming this is provided in your contract or legislated).

In this case, Bruce is shortchanging students and you have evidence in his personnel file of similar kinds of issues in the past. The union needs to see this; otherwise all they will hear is Bruce's version of what has occurred.

This is a vast departure from how such circumstances are typically handled; however, you are still paying union dues and have a right to union protection just as Bruce does. Take advantage of it. Further, if you are on sound ground, and you would not go to this extreme unless you were confident that you are, the meeting with the union may be very brief. Once they review the concern and the information you provide, they may very well tell Bruce that he needs to listen to your expectations and meet them.

In the next meeting with Bruce you need to be very precise about the concerns, expectations, steps to be taken, and follow-up to monitor what will happen in the future.

Remember, you have to make sure that your intervention is effective. This is crucial for a number of reasons: (a) failure to do so means that there is a good chance that you may lose the trust and enthusiasm of

Reluctant and Committed faculty; (b) doing so will provide a clear picture of what you stand for and how far you are willing to go to follow through on your expectations for all faculty; and (c) you have to be able to tell the students, and in some cases parents, that the problem is going to be resolved in a satisfactory manner.

Depending on your contract and practices, you may be going in to observe Bruce's classes. A review of course outlines with all faculty members teaching the research and comp courses should occur. You will not be singling Bruce out, but you will ask everyone to participate by reviewing the course outlines as well as their own syllabi to make sure all involved agree that alignment exists. You also need to let Bruce know that you feel a responsibility to communicate with the concerned students and you will be in touch with them.

When you are done, have lunch with the union representative. You do not need to go into detail about Bruce, but it does not hurt to be clear about what you are trying to accomplish and how you are going about it. Good representatives will often give you helpful advice. Thank them, be consistent, and build trust. They may be able to help you see things from a different perspective, just as you might be able to do the same for them.

EXPLANATION OF ANDREW'S AND BRUCE'S BEHAVIORS

Like most others in the department, Andrew's needs are fulfilled through accomplishment and professionalism. He takes pleasure in quality work, he believes in what he does and his ability to make a difference for the students he serves, and he is highly regarded by students.

Andrew's behaviors are proactive and aimed at problem solving. While supporting him and maintaining his confidence are crucial to you, your response to his problem is not through him, it is through Bruce. Andrew does not require affirmation, but he does require a safe, healthy work environment for himself and the students that the department is serving, and Bruce is depriving him of that. By approaching you, Andrew is reaching out for help.

Bruce, on the other hand, is Passive-Aggressive. As long as he is able to have a comfortable schedule without demands being placed on him by the chair and administration, he will do his best to stay under the radar and remain passive. However, when criticism arises, especially criticism that is supported by hard data, Bruce jumps quickly to aggressive behaviors. His use of sarcasm and walking out of a meeting allow him to avoid reality.

Bruce has witnessed other chairs over the years that either avoided conflict or failed to get support from previous deans when it came to dealing with him. On the rare occasions that he was called on to discuss his performance with someone in authority, avoidance has worked for him. And while he does not know for sure how you are going to respond, he finds it natural to revert to behaviors that have worked successfully for him in the past.

As with most poor performers, Bruce is absolutely aware of his inadequacies. If asked, he would never describe what he does as fun for him. He knows he is a poor teacher. He knows that students generally do not like or respect him. But he has survived in a fur-lined rut that pays him adequately and provides great insurance and retirement benefits, and he knows that it is highly unlikely he could find another job that would compensate him or allow him the time and flexibility that he gets in his present position.

As a result of the world he has built, his power comes from the protection he receives through his contract and the fact that he has not run into university administrators that have demanded changes in his behavior.

The lack of affiliation he receives from most of his peers and students was once painful, but he has determined that what he gets in concrete benefits compensates him for what he loses in psychological benefits. He has found solace from other Resistors. They share many of the same needs as Bruce and find comfort in vilifying the flaws in the system, the leadership, and the students as a way to protect their own inadequacies.

MORE EFFECTIVE MEANS TO ENGAGE BRUCE

Any alterations to Bruce's future behaviors are totally dependent on his willingness to change. Expectations for Bruce have to be clear and rational. He needs to participate in the conversation to develop those expectations. He also needs to be aware that "there may be potential further action" if he fails to resolve the concerns that have been identified. But ultimately, he is the one that has to determine whether he will follow through in spirit as well as in action.

Bruce's style of problem solving becomes public when he exhibits his ability to shift from passive-aggressive to very aggressive behaviors when confronted by facts that make him uncomfortable. At this point, in a follow-up meeting, he is cornered, and while you could take advantage of the position he is in, you shouldn't. The data, and the concerns that you have received from students, provide strong criticism of his practices.

Bruce needs to be given an opportunity to save face, and pounding him into the ground without a means of escape will only result in him focusing on his anger instead of serving students.

The follow-up meeting will be an opportunity to review your concerns in depth. The existing data should not be dismissed or minimized. However, complimenting Bruce on things he has done well over the years is a good first step when the conversation begins to shift to what will occur next.

Some of these next steps might take place cooperatively with all three of the faculty members that teach the course: Bruce, Andrew, and Ronald. This could be approached as a "review" of the program and time might be taken to talk about the syllabus as well as share effective instructional approaches. Jointly, additional options might be identified such as planning together or team-teaching some classes together to assure that everyone is working well together in delivering the curriculum.

While helpful to Bruce, this also allows Andrew and Ronald to see firsthand that you have followed through on your promise to address the concerns that Andrew brought to you. By asking them to help solve the problem by putting in some time with Bruce, they will also become more vested in its solution.

It would be wise for you to also participate in the discussions that take place and share that you will come to classes to observe changes being implemented. Your visibility and involvement send a message as to the importance you attach to this effort.

Personal Reflection

Andrew's approaching you with his concerns reinforces your perception that no problem exists in isolation. Every issue that you address with one person somehow affects others in the department as well. In Bruce's case, students have been immediately affected.

For some it might mean another semester and additional costs. For faculty, it has resulted in anger when students have come to them and begged to be allowed to drop Bruce's section and then be added to their rosters. For past chairs, it meant having to explain to the dean why Bruce had lower class sizes than several of his colleagues.

Failure to confront the problem added to the larger dysfunction that has now become a trademark of the department. Bruce is not the only one to contribute to this, but he certainly is a major factor. As you've learned, each problem, and each individual, is unique. As a result, it further reinforces that you have to deal with each of these challenges one at a time.

Constancy is critical with Bruce. After taking the time to identify clear goals and plans for reaching them, you know you have to regularly monitor Bruce's efforts. You also know that he needs to see you doing this. An old saying puts it well: "What gets monitored, gets done."

TWELVE
Bill: Committed and Angry

"Let us be grateful to people who make us happy, they are the charming gardeners who make our souls blossom."

—Marcel Proust

The recent history of the department has involved four different faculty members in the chair position over the last seven years. Bill had the longest tenure, having put in three years before several of the Resistors made it so difficult for him to continue that he ultimately resigned.

However, through it all Bill continued to be a Committed faculty member. If there was a Most Popular Award voted on by students, he would most likely get it. Bill is devoted to students and even after being displaced as chair, is the go-to person when something needs to be done that is student-related.

Because of his long history in the department he knows how to navigate the waters of upper administration and is well networked throughout the university. And while he has every right to be bitter toward several faculty and the department in general, he has consistently refrained from allowing that to happen.

One of the many activities that Bill has been involved with is the development of the Support Our Kids Program (SOK). SOK is an after-school tutoring program for children from high-need families. It was started through a federal grant during the time that Bill was chair, and he was instrumental in its implementation. The one other faculty member who worked with Bill on obtaining the grant has left and taken another position elsewhere.

As a result, Bill took on the position of SOK Coordinator after he left the department chair position. Because of the program's positive growth, Bill receives three units of release-time from teaching in order to coordinate the program. Bill also has a Program Assistant, Natalie, who oversees the six student tutors that provide services each day to the high school students that come in after their school day has ended for tutoring help.

Midway through your first semester as chair, you are surprised when you receive a telephone call from Bill. He is at the Tutoring Center and three of the student tutors did not report to work, nor did they call in to say they would not be there. Bill tells you that he has called each of them but received no reply. He said that Natalie has no idea what is going on either, but for the moment the two of them are filling in. You find this strange, but you tell Bill to carry on and you will see if you can learn anything more.

Immediately after hanging up you receive a call from the dean's office. Her assistant asks that you come up immediately. Since these calls are extremely uncommon, your radar tells you something is going on and it isn't good. You let your administrative assistant know where you are going and that you may be a while as you quickly depart.

When you reach the dean's office you are ushered right in. The dean has a grimace on her face as she reaches onto her desk to pick up an envelope to hand to you.

Dean: *Here, you need to read this . . .*

You: *Okay.*

You take the envelope as you drop into a chair and begin reading:

Dear Dean,
    We have chosen not to come to work at the Tutoring Center today, and we will not be returning to our positions at the center in the future. We believe we have been sexually harassed by Ms. Natalie and do not feel safe working there.
    From this point forward, please make any contacts with us through our attorney, Mr. Barry Hammer from Service With a Smile, Attorneys at Law.
Sincerely,
Lisa, Alyssa, Maisa

You are shocked. You have had no indication that anything like this might be happening and you share that with the dean.

Dean: *I'm in the same boat. Obviously, we would never knowingly allow anything like this to happen. The fact of the matter is there may or may not be an actual problem. However, our protocol here is to immediately notify HR and have them handle the investigation. Based on what you said, you've had no indication of any problem. So our next step will be to give it to HR, and I'm sure they will be in touch with both of us very quickly.*

True to her word, you receive a call from HR within the hour. You have learned over the years that anything that may involve a potential lawsuit gets quick attention. You give Ezra, the assistant director of HR, a review of what has happened thus far, and he asks you to set up a meeting with him, you, and Bill at 5:00 p.m., after the Tutoring Center has closed for the day and students have left.

The 5:00 p.m. meeting is brief since there is not a lot of new information that has not already been covered. Ezra asks Bill a number of questions about Natalie:

How long has she worked there?

Have there ever been any previous complaints about her?

What is the physical layout of the Tutoring Center like?

Have any of these girls ever complained to you about Natalie before? Has anyone else?

Have you witnessed any behaviors by Natalie related to these kinds of situations?

Are there any offices in the building that are not visible to people standing outside?

Does Natalie have access to a computer and, if so, where is it located?

Who supervises her?

What are her work hours?

How often is she alone with tutors and students?

He also asks for a copy of her personnel file. You and Bill respond to Ezra's questions and promise to get him the personnel materials he wants before leaving. Ezra thanks both of you and tells Bill that he needs to talk with you privately for a minute. At this point, Bill leaves the room.

Ezra asks you again to confirm that the Tutoring Center is closed for the day. Once you do that, he tells you that he wants you to take him and a member of the Administrative Technology Department to the Tutoring Center so that a copy of Natalie's hard drive can be made and reviewed. He also tells you that he wants to go to Bill's office after that and do the same thing with his computer. Further, he tells you that he will be in touch with the dean, who will be directed to contact Natalie and let her know that an investigation is taking place and that she is not to come onto campus until she is notified.

You get into contact with the dean after Ezra has left to say you are in shock. But you are particularly concerned that Bill's hard drive is being checked. You point out that there was nothing in the letter about Bill and, to be honest, you find this action offensive. You let the dean know that if it was up to you, you would be extremely angry. The dean points out that this is not personal; it is part of a standard operating process that HR follows, and regardless of who was involved, including the provost or president, they would be treated the same way.

While you have a great deal of confidence in the dean, you have a hard time visualizing the president's hard drive being viewed; however, this one is not in your control. You know from her tone that the dean is not happy about this either, but there are times that everyone has to follow directives and this is just one of those instances.

The next morning you are notified that inappropriate material was found on Natalie's computer. You are also told that Bill's computer was fine, but that Natalie will be formally suspended pending further investigation.

As the investigation proceeds, the university does indeed get served notice from Attorney Hammer and the Service With a Smile Law Firm. The Commissioner of Higher Education's office handles these legal affairs, not the local campus. However, Human Resources asks you to sit in with the attorney from the commissioner's office when he questions Natalie and the three young women to prepare for a potential trial.

During the course of the interviews with the three tutors, it becomes apparent that Natalie did things that were inappropriate. However, the tutors made it clear that neither Bill, nor the chair, nor any other faculty or staff member were present when these events took place.

Eventually a settlement is reached, and you believe the matter has been brought to closure. There will not be a trial. The young women each received a sum of money, and Natalie decided to resign from her position before the university took any action.

However, a week later a letter from the office of the Vice President for Human Resources shows up in your mailbox. You open it and find that it is a copy. The original was sent to Bill, notifying him that he is being reprimanded for failing to appropriately supervise his Tutoring Center staff. While he is not being suspended or fined, copies of the letter have been sent to the chair, dean, president, and his personnel file. Before you have a chance to process the whole thing, Bill walks into your office with his copy of the letter in his hand.

> Bill: *Are you kidding me? Are you kidding? Did you see this? The Vice President of HR sent me a letter of reprimand for what Natalie did? You know that those girls were asked very directly about whether or not I ever said or did anything, and they all said I didn't. They all said that she was always careful to pull her stupid acts when I wasn't around. Why in the hell am I getting a letter?*
>
> *You know, I was hurt and quite honestly angry as hell when they searched my computer. But I accepted it and went along. But this, this is absolutely not acceptable. I'm resigning from my position with the Center, and for that matter I am resigning from every committee I am on. We've got jackasses working here who screw students as well as their colleagues and they get away with it. I do everything I can to contribute and then I get this? The hell with this place. I've had it.*

There are few people in the university that you respect more than Bill. When the dean noted her discomfort with checking his hard drive, you did not like it, either but you understood it. Fortunately, at the time, Bill accepted it as well. However, this is completely different. This is a person with integrity who has done everything he could for the sake of the students and the program. You know you need time to think this through, and you know that you need to be very careful of what you are about to say because you are not sure where this is going to go next.

For the moment, you put your hand on his shoulder and let him know that you fully understand why he feels the way he does. You add that you would feel the same way if you were in his shoes. You ask him if he wants to go home and let him know that you will cover his classes if he does. (Note: You will cover it personally, not someone else.) You also ask him to try to hold himself together and let him know you want to look into this further.

When you took this position it was with the attitude that you had nothing to lose. You are not looking to make a move into administration or further your career. Your only interest was in helping the department to get to a point where its members could function reasonably well.

However, after a lot of reflection, discussion with the dean and your best advisor, your wife, and a near-sleepless night, you come to a conclusion: Quite simply, you truly do not believe that Bill did anything wrong. You know that the letter from HR was at the direction of the attorney in the Commissioner's Office, a woman located almost one hundred miles away from your campus who knows nothing about Bill and his contributions to the university. You also wonder, if the attorney was away from her office and her administrative assistant touched a student worker in the office, would she suspend herself? The whole thing is unfair and absurd.

There is a popular saying, "Is this the hill you want to die on?" There is not much that occurs on campuses that is so serious that it cannot be fixed or, if necessary, dubiously accepted. But this case is different. When you think about situations like this, you find that it is really helpful to think about it happening to a member of your family. So if Bill was your father, how would you respond? Would you say it was understandable since he is the supervisor of the person? Quite simply, no, you wouldn't. You sit down at your computer and type a letter. Following this you call the dean's secretary and ask for an appointment.

The dean welcomes you to her office at 4:15 p.m. It is near the end of the day and most of the faculty and students have left. The only ones still on campus are the staff who are ending their day and a handful of professors who are teaching evening classes.

Dean: *I'd offer you something with alcohol, but the good old days of being able to do that are over. Coffee? Water?*

You: *No, thanks. Look, I really appreciate and value our relationship. As you know, I've willingly handled a lot of ugly stuff this year and haven't complained about it or asked for anything special. But this situation with Bill, for the first time since I've been in this role, I have to tell you that this is out of line. It's unacceptable, and I am not going to work for an administration that would do this. Either the letter gets pulled, or I am going to have to step down.*

The dean looks at you for a long moment. She does not say a word but then reaches over and picks up her phone.

Dean: *I need to see him now. It's very important.*

She is put on hold for a moment.

Okay. We will be right over.

Dean (to you): *Come on.*

You: *Where are we going?*

Dean: *To the power tower.*

When you enter the provost's office his tie is off, his sleeves are rolled up, and his gray and brown, shaggy senior-citizen dog of unknown heredity is sitting on his leather couch.

Provost: *I'd tell him to move, but he doesn't listen to me. Much like everybody else around here. Sit down, grab a chair. I'd ask you what's up, but I think I have a pretty good idea.*

Since you were not really prepared for this meeting, you tell yourself that your best strategy right now is to keep your mouth shut. The dean was the one that put this together, so best to let her speak.

Dean: *I have a professor who has probably done more for our college over the years than anyone else, and he's getting jerked around by an attorney who visits our campus at best once every five years. And even if she doesn't want to consider his contributions, the way this whole thing has played out is unfair just based on its merits.*

We've got a couple of thousand support personnel working at this university every day. Are you telling me if a repairman who works in a dozen different buildings during the day, or a landscaper who spends the entire day outside, or a secretary whose boss is not in the office over 50 percent of the time, were to say or do something out of line, that their supervisors would deserve to be disciplined?

Look boss, we have all taken the sexual harassment course and we regularly supervise the people under us, but we cannot live with them 24/7. Do you know what your assistants are looking at on their computers at this very moment?

Provost: *I hear what you are saying, and I see the unfairness. Let me think about this one.*

The provost looks at you and asks if there is anything you want to add. In a very even, calm, and measured voice you respond.

You: *I don't have a lot to add, but I have thought this through. You've known me a long time, and you know I don't jump off the handle or act irrationally or out of passion. But I have to tell you, this one is simply wrong. We cannot afford to lose this guy's trust. If we are ever going to rebuild the mess in this department, he's one of the handful of people that we need to provide a foundation. You allow this to happen and you're going to lose him, you're going to lose some of the other good professors that we count on, and with all due respect, you're going to lose your present chair.*

The room is quiet as the provost mulls over your statement before he responds: *OK. I fully understand that this is not a knee-jerk reaction. Let me think about it. I will get back to you shortly, I promise, because I don't want to let this hang.*

The dean thanks you for coming and asks you to wait outside while she stays to talk further with the provost. The dog raises her head, opens one eye, and yawns as you exit. After a few minutes the dean enters the waiting area and nods to you. You get up and walk outside with her. As you head back toward your building, the dean suggests stopping in the campus Rathskellar. This is a first.

Dean, as you order your drink: *Beer? I thought you were a wine guy.*

You: *Normally, yeah. But I needed something with a little more body to it today.*

The dean smiles. *Just so you know, we may be team-teaching together.*

You: *I'm not with you. Team-teaching?*

Dean: *Yup. After you left, I told the provost that for the first time in my career, I have witnessed something that I absolutely cannot live with. There's no way I can call Bill in and justify this. I may be a stuffed shirt, but underneath that shirt I'd like to think I still stand for something. I told him either the letter gets pulled or I'm back on faculty with you. I also told him I'd make a compromise: I'd apologize to Bill on behalf of the administration. Rest assured, the attorney in the Commissioner's Office isn't going to do it.*

You smile for the first time in the last two days: *Wow, pretty courageous.*

Dean: *Actually, nah. He'll agree.*

You: *You really think so?*

Dean: *I'd bet money on it. Who else would ever take these jobs? He can't afford to lose us!*

She laughs. *I'm kidding. In reality, the provost has integrity. As long as I've known him, he's always done the right thing because it was the right thing to do. Watch, he'll call Bill in and toss the letter in the basket in front of him and mollify him. I'm not saying Bill won't be angry—he has a right to be. But in the end the damning letter will get pulled, and you and I will work hard to let him know that he has our backing.*

EXPLANATION OF BILL'S BEHAVIOR

Bill's case differs from his department colleagues in that his major concern at this point is not with Resistors on the faculty but with the university's administration. While disheartened by some of the treatment that he received in the past, he is one of those rare individuals who appreciates all of the positive gifts he has received in life and is able to move forward, even through some of the very difficult times he has experienced.

Bill sincerely likes students. He likes teaching. He likes the life of a professor. You are also aware that he holds some deep religious beliefs. Because of all this, he has refused to succumb to the negativism that has surrounded him due to colleagues who lack the same ability to choose positive over negative.

However, even for Bill there is a breaking point. To him, the perception of rampant unfairness is not acceptable. When this situation occurs, none of his basic psychological needs in terms of enjoyment, power, or affiliation are being met whatsoever. He feels threatened, angry, and humiliated to think that with all of his dedication to the university, he could be treated in this way.

While Bill's case is different from most of the others you have dealt with so far in terms of root causes, the effects have the potential to be the same. The enthusiasm of arguably your strongest faculty member could be lost. Further, because of the immense respect he has received over the years, other Committed and Reluctant faculty, both in the department and outside of it, may observe this case and also lose trust in the leadership at the college as well as the university level. This is not lost on the dean, and she realizes that this is one of the rare cases where her behavior will also be judged by others in the academy.

MORE EFFECTIVE MEANS TO ENGAGE BILL

When you reflect on what either you or Bill might have done differently, you cannot identify anything that he did that was critically in error. The Commissioner's Office and campus administration were responsible for this. It is true that supervisors have responsibility for their subordinates. That does not mean, however, that the total picture should be ignored. After investigating, you are convinced that Bill did everything reasonable to supervise and maintain a professional office. His many years of service with an unblemished record further support his reputation. The attorney failed to look into all of this and consider it. As a result, she made an expedient determination and then moved on to her next case, leaving you to clean up the mess.

At this point, it is not a matter of what Bill could have done different-ly. It is a matter of you, the dean, provost, and university taking respon-sibility to work with Bill and others in supervisory positions to look at how supervision takes place and what might be done differently to pre-vent such instances from happening again. However, no matter how much training you do, you can never guarantee that such instances can be completely avoided.

Personal Reflection

Since Bill's case involved non-instructional staff members and the commissioner's office, it was different than the cases you dealt with pre-viously. As a problem solver, you know there are few instances in which you cannot find a creative solution. But in this case the system's adminis-tration acted without involving local leadership.

If you overplay your cards by threatening to quit your job every time you do not like a decision, you will eventually find yourself to be the most noble person in the unemployment line. However, once or twice in your career you may witness a case in which someone is treated so egre-giously that you find it absolutely unacceptable. When this occurs, you either surrender or act.

What is important is that you are fully aware of the consequences of your actions and you have no doubt that you can live with them. If acting hastily may put you out of a job with no way to make a mortgage pay-ment, feed your family, and pay your bills, you might want to wait to hand in that letter of resignation.

Timing is everything, and in your case since you still hold your status as a faculty member, you are comforted knowing you can return to your teaching position and will not lose any sleep over your decision. More courageous is the decision of the dean, who let the provost know that she was also willing to give up her more prestigious position based on princi-ple. For her, aspirations to move to the next level of administration would likely be dashed if in fact she really followed through with her threat.

THIRTEEN

The Year Ends

"Does anybody really think that they didn't get what they had because they didn't have the talent or the strength or the endurance or the commitment?"
—Nelson Mandela

Classes ended two weeks ago, and today is the last day of final exams. You marvel as you walk to the library to pick up some books and articles that you want to read during the summer break. The hustle and bustle of the final weeks, with students filling the hallways to prepare for final exams, has suddenly converted those same corridors to a quiet ghost town.

Keeping up with your own discipline has been pretty much impossible over the last year, and you look forward to the opportunity to catch up on some reading. The demands of returning to the department chair position have been extremely challenging and time consuming.

You cannot get over the way bureaucracy has multiplied since you were last in the position. The state seems to change credentialing requirements every year or two. That's bad enough, but the changes are almost meaningless. They appear to say the same things but with different words and in a different order.

And now it has become your job to convince faculty that it is important for them to sacrifice time from preparing to teach and serve students. Instead they will have to give their attention to hundreds of hours on committees filling out forms for bureaucrats looking for ways to keep themselves busy.

Having spent enough time in the academy, you have learned to accept this reality, though you have never accepted liking it. On top of these demands, the more immediate responsibility—to try to guide your department back to some state of normalcy—has been on your own front

129

burner. Unfortunately, your ability to read and research and write in any depth has been pretty much curtailed.

A LITTLE OLDER, A LITTLE WISER

As you mull all this over, you think about how much has happened in just one year. The first thing that comes to mind is the discussions that took place when your colleagues and the dean approached you to take the chair position, and the conversation you then had with your wife. You have always appreciated your spouse's support for your work.

But you realize now, more than ever, how hard this job would be without the understanding she has shown over the last year. Your ability to help around the house and handle a lot of the chores that you did in the past has been limited by the responsibilities of your job.

You know that at times your mind was on some event at school when you should have been listening to something she was saying to you. When the phone rings in the evening and you see that the call originates from a number at the university your heart cannot help but skip a beat, wondering if there is a crisis that you are going to have to handle.

While you are sensitive to the fact that all of this comes with the job, and you are aware that fellow chairs throughout the university share what you are experiencing, you also know that it would be impossible for you to fulfill your responsibilities effectively without the support you get from home.

You have also learned how important it has been for you to get adequate sleep and to have a good diet. One of the most important pieces of advice that a fellow chair gave you was to take out a gym membership. By stopping several mornings each week and doing some cardio and easy weight lifting and stretching, you have found a new source of energy. When you look around the room during some of the late afternoon meetings you are required to attend, you see a lot of people struggling to keep their eyes open. The fitness boost you have added by taking better care of yourself has really been a big help.

Thinking back to the time when you first became a chair versus your present situation, you realize that these supports, while important and helpful, are not nearly enough to assist you in performing your duties as well as you need to. This time around there is also a mental health side to the job that most people are completely unaware of. Working with a number of dysfunctional individuals is emotionally draining. When you see instances of students being provided poor instruction or supervision or counseling, it is heart wrenching.

While you hear a lot of people making fun of the new generation of millennials, the vast majority of students you work with are struggling to pay for their education and help support their families. They are hungry to learn, get their degrees, and find secure jobs. They deserve the best we can give them.

In addition, when you observe some faculty members refusing to interact with peers, aggressively attacking them in meetings, or sabotaging them behind their backs, it is disheartening to think professionals could behave this way.

You now realize why the dean made the decision to hire you. While you are a member of the department and will have to continue to work with these people after you leave the chair position, you also know that no one who is just starting out in leadership could take this position. They would be destroyed. Outsiders were unable to come in and get the job done, and so that really left you as the obvious choice. She believed that your skin was thick enough to handle the jabs and digs.

At the same time, she did everything she reasonably could to provide you with protections. The faculty was incapable of meeting together, so she guaranteed there would be no large group meetings, and this kept you from being put in a position in which havoc might ensue. She also responded to pretty much every request you made, from small but symbolic gestures like the physical renovation of the office to more important personnel decisions involving instances in which you had to institute disciplinary procedures against some individuals who violated contractual, procedural, or legal requirements.

The most important thing the dean provided you with was trust. As you pondered this concept when you first started back on the job, you observed it as something that developed as a result of time and consistency. You had told her that you would need her backing with critical decisions that you had to make. You pointed out that you would confer with her first before anything important came down, but that there might be times when you had to make decisions in the "here and now," and you expected her to trust you if that happened.

She consistently did so, and that was incredibly important to you, not just in dealing with the matters at hand but in knowing that she had your back. This relieved a huge amount of potential mental strain. Without her support, you know that you would not even be thinking about continuing on for another year, because you could not do the job without it.

As you reflect on what you observed in dealing with each of the dysfunctional faculty members you were faced with over the year, you realize that one of the most important things that you learned was the need for a strong relationship of trust between people in leadership positions.

This is something you will keep in your back pocket and refer to in the future if you ever do change your career path and decide to look at another leadership role. Whether you are looking for a job or considering someone to work with you, you will ask yourself whether the person you will be depending on is someone who you believe you can trust.

The Year Unfolded

It was an interesting time. As you reflect, you realize that many people tested you during this period, much like children test boundaries of parents, or kids test limits with teachers.

Resistors

You have no doubt that many of the Resistors truly believed it would be business as usual. They had seen several chairs appointed in recent years, and by manifesting their Reluctant-related behaviors, they were able to maintain instability and do the things that they wanted to do.

You knew you had to deal with some confusion when initially planning how to handle Resistors. On the one hand, you wanted to give everyone a chance to start with a clean record in hopes that perhaps with you in the role as a new chair, they would respond differently. On the other, you did not feel it was fair to simply ignore past infractions of people who did things that were out of line.

Your ultimate decision—to try to give everyone a chance for a fresh start but at least read their personnel files in case problems were to arise—ended up making a lot of sense. There were times that your knowledge of past behaviors on the part of some individuals was helpful as you met and worked with those persons.

The use of progressive discipline was also valuable. It gave you a structured and consistent procedure to use when necessary. The HR office was able to provide training in this concept, and it was helpful when Anthony accused you of harassing him when some incidents occurred and you had to write him up for failing to provide appropriate supervision to fieldwork students. You had records of complaints from students and supervising teachers, as well as a copy of notes you made related to a conversation that the two of you had on this topic. Those notes were further supported by the follow-up email you sent Anthony after the conversation took place.

Over time, Anthony, Antoine, Bruce, and Mary all realized that you were going to maintain a level of expectations in terms of their professional responsibilities as well as personal conduct and hold them to it. This did not increase their level of enjoyment for the job. It also reduced their sense of power. They knew they were not going to dominate you in terms of their control over their positions. You made it clear that communications regarding departmental practices needed to be transparent and consistent.

Further, you regularly emphasized that students were to be treated in a respectful manner. All professors were expected to meet with classes on time. No one was to simply cancel a class unless there was an emergency and without checking with you first. Papers were to be read and handed back with comments, where appropriate. Procedures for supervising and counseling were to be met as outlined in the current department handbooks that were developed by the faculty.

While none of these expectations were unreasonable, they were not happening on a consistent basis over the last several years. Refreshing everyone's memories of these expectations, supervising to make sure they took place, and recognizing faculty members who performed well has helped you and other proactive members of the department to begin to build a new culture.

Mary has actually been more positive in participating in committees and volunteering to help with curriculum initiatives that will provide value to the department in the future.

Antoine, while not happy with the changes, has decided to meet expectations. He does what is necessary, not so much because of his love for students, but more because he does not want to face the negative consequences from the chair. While you would always prefer to see behavioral change as a result of positive reinforcement rather than negative, you've learned to take what you can get.

Anthony has decided that the headaches were not worth it. Having met the basic requirements for retirement, he handed in his resignation and is moving to a nearby state that does not have a state income tax. The last you heard he is planning to sell organic vegetables at local farmers' markets.

Bruce has actually become more positive and willing to work with Ronald and Andrew in reviewing the syllabus and methods for the Research courses. Bruce was a good example of a once effective teacher who became caught up in the deterioration of the department. Not a strong individual personally, he became aligned with other Resistors and followed their leads. Your suggestion that Bruce and the union representative talk was probably the most effective action you could take in his case.

You made it clear to Bruce that new norms were being established and maintained. When the union representative saw the data and some of his course materials, he made it clear to Bruce that his work would be very difficult to defend if a hearing were to take place. Further, rumor has it that the union rep simply told Bruce that he should be embarrassed by his performance and to get his act together.

As a senior faculty member, Anthony had a great deal of influence on Bruce and others. He was involved in personnel decisions affecting many of the other faculty. New faculty did not want to challenge him, and so when he used sarcasm in meetings, publicly ostracized administration, and modeled bad habits in the way he treated students, no one was willing to call him on it, including past chairs and deans.

This behavior became a virus. Others, like Bruce, saw it and in some cases replicated parts of it: "If Anthony can cancel classes before the holidays, why can't I?" "If Anthony can ignore students by simply giving them smiley faces on papers, why can't I?"

While most other faculty did not replicate Anthony's actions, individuals did pick up on certain behaviors, and as you look back you now see the slow deterioration of the healthy culture that once existed. And further, while Anthony seemed to lead the pack, it was not just him. It also included other Resistors who fed into the change that had occurred over the years, but more importantly, it involved former chairs and deans that contributed to the erosion.

When you spoke to one former chair, she told you that she had called several Resistors into her office for discussions of their behaviors during her term, but when she went to Human Resources and tried to take actions to initiate some counseling letters (an early step in progressive discipline), she was not given support.

Likewise, complaints to the office of a former dean resulted in the same refusal to act. She recalled how once that happened she lost all control. It became clear to the Resistors that she was no more than a paper lion, a figurehead with no teeth. Obviously, if former administration had taken reasonable actions at that time, there is a very good chance you would not be here at this time.

Reluctants

As you think about Jennifer, Andrew, and Sandy, you take a deep breath, look up to the sky, and whisper, "Thank you."

All three of these faculty members are great teachers and contributors. If there was one major theme related to your efforts, it was protection. Interestingly, the protection took different forms. With Jennifer, it was a very basic matter of safety. In her case, she felt threatened by Resistors who might harm her opportunities for reappointment and tenure.

In Andrew's case, it was his perception that he, as well as other faculty, were not being treated fairly and equitably. Andrew felt the same inherent need for fairness that most of us feel. With the appointment of a new chair, he believed this was a "do or die" time. Either the practices that had been taking place over the last few years were going to end, or he was ready to bail out. By stepping up, you have given Andrew hope that things in fact will be different and a change in the culture is truly possible.

Protecting Sandy took a different form. As a long-term, tenured, and highly respected faculty member, Sandy was seen by most people in the university as the classic successful professor. And in many ways he was.

However, Sandy was intimidated by Anthony and other Resistors. He was fearful of breaking from them because it might end personal relationships. It also might leave him alone in the department. He was not sure if he would be able to cultivate other supportive relationships. In addition, he had a history with many of the Resistors just based on their years together. By making the decision to eliminate Anthony from the summer program, you have taken the pressure off of Sandy. You were able to play the "bad guy."

Sandy, and some of the other Reluctants who felt this social pressure, caused you to look at the future of the department in the long run. Anthony's sudden announced retirement has already lessened a lot of tension. As a very strong negative influence, his departure has signaled a certain relief for a number of people. And self-admittedly, knowing that he would not be there did cause you to go into your office, close the door, do a fist pump, and say, "YES!"

Committed

Committed faculty were affected by the departure of Anthony as well. One made a comment, overheard as he poured a cup of coffee in the office the day after Anthony's announcement: "Thank goodness, maybe things will be different around here now." While you agreed with this observation, you were surprised at how much negative influence one toxic individual could have on an entire department.

It was not so much that he directly influenced the lives of so many other faculty members, but it was the indirect and subtle comments and behaviors that had provided much of the negative culture over the years.

When you first started this appointment, you assumed that Committed faculty would be the easiest to manage. After all, they were already aligned with the right values and goals. And while this was true to some extent, it was not quite as simple as you thought it would be. Working with this group provided you with as many insights into leading and managing as working with the Resistors and Reluctants.

Wanda was the easiest, but also perhaps the most fragile. You love her directness, clear understanding of what we are supposed to be about, and courage. Though a young, new member, she had no compunction about coming to you to resolve the issue threatening her grant. And while addressing this particular issue was a challenge for you, it was simple and clear for Wanda.

In this case, her desires and yours were compatible and your actions resolved her concerns involving Sandy. If they had not, Wanda is talented and confident enough to walk away from the project and possibly even the university and look for another position elsewhere if she does not feel she is being supported.

Wanda could be a "hothead" if not handled well. You realize, moving forward, that while she is a potentially great asset, she could be difficult under different circumstances as well. Because of this you make a note to yourself that you need to spend more time with her and help her gain a better understanding of how decisions are made and the fact that none of us get what we want all of the time.

Bill is at the other end of the spectrum. Where Wanda is a strong, new Committed, Bill is a strong, veteran Committed who has had his faith shaken. Interestingly, the situation he was involved in has been disturbing, not only for him but also for you.

Bill has been the face of the department for years. Even through some of the difficult times in recent years, he has provided a moral compass as well as been a role model. He has done his best to contribute as an instructor and as a chair. Even after being dismissed from the chair position, he has acted with dignity and continued to do good work. The situation over the last year involving his assistant was more than he could handle.

Even though the provost backed off on the disciplinary action taken against him, Bill was so personally affronted by what occurred that he swore he would never trust the central administration or the commissioner's office again. He fully appreciated the support that you and the dean provided, but he has made it clear that his days of volunteering and doing anything that would be above and beyond normal job duties are at an end.

You are hopeful that with time Bill will mellow and return to being the person that you have known over the years. Whether that will happen or not, you aren't sure. This situation causes you to recall the advice you read in a leadership book that suggested that people who are closest to the action are typically the best ones to make decisions.

You and the dean were right on with this one. The chancellor's office was myopic, and their narrow view has caused a good professor to lose much of his spirit. The provost's willingness to allow this to happen only exacerbated the problem. This leaves it up to you and the college to try to nurture him back. As with so many others, only time will tell.

SUMMARY

While the characters portrayed are fictionalized, parts of them come from experiences and stories shared by chairs and professors who have operated in higher education. However, no one individual presented is intended to portray a specific person from real life.

A rough definition of the law of entropy suggests that a mass left alone cannot remain in its present state—it either deteriorates or it moves forward. This can be translated from science to management when we look at how departments in higher education operate. The once-healthy Department of Secondary Education described here had slowly deteriorated into a dysfunctional mess. No one woke up one day and saw this occur as the result of a switch being turned from "on" to "off." Rather, it had been a slow, insipient process, usually the result of one or two personalities that absorbed others along the way.

None of the groups that we have witnessed are one defined, bounded group within a department. Sometimes there are subsets. At times individuals move back and forth from one group to another as well as across groups, depending on the issue and personalities involved. The process is neither clear nor linear. It's messy and always changing.

What also became apparent in speaking with veteran faculty members from higher education is that a "great department" can become marginalized in very short order. This has been known to occur when a chair with a Committed personality leaves and a chair with a following of Resistors takes over. New practices that favor one group over another in a department can cause anger and division. Funneling opportunities to make extra money or giving choice classes to friends were examples that were cited.

Likewise, instances of difficult contract negotiations have at times caused long-lasting resentments. When the union keeps telling faculty members that they are not appreciated, that they are seen as second-class citizens by administration, some faculty actually believe what they hear, and when the negotiations are over they cannot let go of it.

The message that came across regularly from veteran leaders in discussing their own experiences is to never take anything for granted. Just like personal relationships, the health of a department or any other unit needs to be constantly fed and nurtured.

To get past these kinds of challenges and foster positive working environments, leaders in higher education need to recognize goals and behaviors that their institutions value and have in common. They need to make sure that all persons involved—administration, faculty, staff, and students—clearly understand what those goals and behaviors are and work with constancy and predictability toward meeting them.

Agreed-upon goals need to be made public. They need to be recognized when developing programs, developing budgets, doing long-range planning, and perhaps most importantly, in modeling everyday behavior. When these kinds of behaviors are acted out daily, consistently, and predictably, we enhance the possibility of shedding the cloak of dysfunction for one of trust.

FOURTEEN

Five Years Later

"A boss knows how. A leader shows how."

—Shayle Uroff

This book began by laying out a scenario involving a dysfunctional department in a comprehensive university. What I have learned from talking with peers, along with personal experience, is that these kinds of challenging behaviors play out in institutions of higher education every year across the nation. And while the actors may change, the drama and the heartache remain, often affecting not only the professors responsible for them, but also the students that they have been charged with serving.

Throughout this book I have attempted to offer reflections and insights as I depicted the struggles of this fictitious department. In order to provide some final thoughts and a semblance of summary, I have taken the liberty of ending this portion of the book in the same manner that much of it was written—through a conversation between the dean and chair.

Five years after the events described in this book took place, the dean and chair have each transitioned into career opportunities at new universities. The former dean has become provost at a large Midwestern public university. The former chair decided to take a position with a prestigious private college in the southeast. They happen to run into each other at a large annual conference being held in Washington, DC.

Although they have corresponded with each other over the intervening years, their new leadership roles have caused them to reflect on their collaborative experiences, gained all those years ago when they worked together. The two of them set a date to meet for dinner to catch up. Invariably, the discussion turns to their time together dealing with the Secondary Education Department.

Former Chair: *It's good to see you after all this time. How do you like your new job? Is it drama-free? Have you had the opportunity to use any of the interventions we employed back when we worked together?*

Former Dean: *Well, I have to say that after all of these years, our experience was not a unique one. Our description of faculty as falling into one of three groups has for the most part held true, not just at my new university, but also in the stories I hear from colleagues at conferences just like this one.*

However, I have come to believe that no one faculty member falls cleanly into one of the categories; instead, many of them fit into multiple categories and they transition in and out of these classifications over the course of their careers, as well as during the course of particular situations.

Former Chair: *I guess I can validate what you say. Based on my experiences, it's the same here. It has been interesting to see that many of the behaviors we witnessed seem to have a universal quality to them. The whole notion of faculty who tend to remain committed to the mission of the university, those who resist working in unison, and those who are outright reluctant to be engaged in activities that would move programs forward seems to be pretty universal.*

Former Dean: *Yes, for sure. However, like we previously learned, I've noticed that there is quite a bit of movement in individual faculty across this continuum. But I've definitely learned that one's destiny is not set; in other words, a Reluctant can become a Committed, given the right supports and coaching. And while it's rare, I've even seen a handful of Resistors who decided to dig themselves out of the ruts they were in to become productive contributors. The key to this is that you have to give them the benefit of the doubt and the opportunity to do it.*

It has also become apparent to me that personnel in administrative or semi-administrative roles must be very sensitive to faculty who start to become disengaged from the core business of the department, college, or university. I've learned to be much more aware of the need to look for signs of that kind of dysfunction and try to address individuals as quickly as possible. While what we went through provided challenges and was painful at times, it also was a learning experience that has been useful to me as I have gone on in my career.

Former Chair: *I have to agree with you on that observation, as well. It's sad to see faculty following trajectories that maximize disengagement with their work at the university.*

But, at some level, we should think about significant opportunities in developing human capacity for faculty to be productive throughout the entire course of their careers in higher education. Assistant professors are not all alike, and neither are full professors. And for that matter, neither are chairs and deans.

I wonder what might have happened at our previous university if we had a more targeted professional development series in place to support faculty and administrators at all stages of their careers.

Former Dean: *Right on. At my current university, we have designed a program aimed at doing this. Although the final results are still not in, it is showing promise in keeping Committed faculty at that end of the spectrum, and warding off temptations to move into the realms of the Resistant or the Reluctant.*

One key feature of this series is a heightened focus on leadership as personnel move along the trajectory of retention, promotion, and tenure, and affording multiple opportunities for faculty to serve in increasingly involved leadership roles as they progress in their careers. The important element here is that faculty are not simply moved into roles as department chairs; instead, we have developed a series of options for faculty to serve as leaders in the community, on the campus, and at the system level.

Former Chair: *That's great. And what about your existing chairs and deans? Are you doing anything with them? This sounds like an interesting idea that might hold promise at my current institution as well.*

Former Dean: *I know from our many conversations that we both learned a lot dealing with that one particular department. However, wouldn't it have been great if someone had given us some insights and coaching along the way that might have helped us to avoid some of the pitfalls we faced?*

I've come to look at the development process at the college in three tiers. The first is what we just talked about, identifying individuals who may be going off course and trying to address their needs as quickly as possible. This may be as simple as just talking to them and helping them problem-solve a particular issue in their lives: boredom with their job, money problems, family concerns, or health issues, just to name a few.

Sometimes it's more complex than that, and counseling or other services may be appropriate. We have also had our folks in leadership positions get some training in how to listen and respond. This has been very successful.

The second tier involves people in groups. We provide orientation sessions throughout the first two years for our new hires. They meet every couple of months with others who have recently joined us to talk about adjusting to the institution and the demands of the job. We have chairs and deans, and even the provost and president, meet with them for Q and A sessions. This has been very productive for a lot of new folks, both professionally and personally.

We have done similar things for our veteran faculty with periodic breakfast meetings where people share ideas and programs. A lot of good collaborations have come from this.

The third tier is focused on people in leadership roles. As we have shared so many times before, there is no formal training required for higher education positions and too many universities fail to provide good professional development for people who take on these roles. In addition to a summer program hosted by Human Resources, we have one training-related agenda item on each of our monthly meetings for chairs.

In addition, the chairs and their dean have a luncheon every other month and there is no strict agenda. It's a "chairs luncheon" and not a "dean's luncheon." Because of that, the chairs are asked to take the initiative to come up with topics that are important to them. Sometimes they all read an article ahead of time and discuss it. Sometimes they ask to have a speaker from a different division in the college come in and share an idea or program. The key concept is that this is a time for sharing and building community.

How about you? As you think back, is there anything you would have done differently based on what you know now?

Former Chair: *One thing I know is that I would have involved the provost more in the plan of action that I developed. We had a supportive provost. But once we got heavily involved, in some instances it became apparent very quickly that the issues were sometimes much more serious than I anticipated. It would have been a big help to know that he would have been fully supportive if I saw a need for a suspension or a dismissal.*

I know he heard things from you, but you were like family to him. I think if he had heard about a couple of serious concerns from both of us over a period of time, he would have felt more vested in those cases and been more likely to support a tough decision. As it was, I never knew for sure if he would be on my side if called upon, and that made me hesitate at times. I've seen deans and chairs put themselves on the line and then get hung out to dry by upper administration. Once that happens, the dean or chair loses all of their authority in the eyes of faculty.

When the chips were down in Bill's case and he came through. However, his initial decision to allow the letter was costly, and I don't think he truly understood how devastating that was to a really good faculty member. It never should have happened in the first place. If I had a closer relationship with him, it might not have happened.

In the end, everything turned out relatively well. We accomplished what we wanted insofar as the department was functioning by the time you left for your next job. No one would award it a blue ribbon, and a lot of the underlying feelings continued to exist, but the department at least functioned at a reasonable level.

Former Dean: *How long did you stay on?*

Former Chair: *I stayed two more years after you departed. Things improved enough that I got to the point that I looked forward to going to school in the mornings and I felt we were accomplishing some good things. Also, we could not afford to have both of us leave at the same time. That kind of gap in leadership could have been deadly. Some of the Resistors would have jumped on the opportunity to revert back to their old behaviors if there was no one there to maintain the culture that we had worked so hard to resurrect.*

That's something else to be considered if you run into a similar situation in the future. Continuity and consistency are critical. There is no doubt in my mind that the leadership gaps that the department witnessed prior to my appointment had a lot to do with the dysfunctional behaviors that emerged. I think a smart dean has to constantly be thinking about who the next chairs might be in any of his or her departments and begin grooming that leadership, because you know that sooner or later there will be openings.

It's been great having a chance to talk about the old days as well as discuss how we can take what we've learned and use it as we move forward. I really appreciate some of the useful ideas you've shared. So how about you? Let me ask you one last question. If you were going to give advice to other folks like us who were put into leadership positions in challenging climates, what would you tell them?

The dean thought for a moment and looked up with a smile.

Former Dean: *I think it's the greatest job in the world. It's also one of the toughest. Not the toughest — there are a lot of people who deal with much more challenging problems than we do — but still, it's hard. However, there's an old saying, "If you want to experience the peaks, you have to be willing to take the valleys."*

I think what I would say to them is this: First, changing the behavior of adults is extremely difficult. Not impossible, but close to it. However, when you take on a job like the ones that we've been in, you go in with the idea that you are going to do everything you reasonably can to change unproductive behaviors. If the people you are dealing with choose not to make those changes, that's on them, not you.

I've seen people in leadership beat themselves up because individuals they supervised could not be turned around, and that's absurd. They are adults and it's not up to you or me or anyone else to bend the organization to meet their needs. Do you have to be reasonable and understanding? Of course, but there also have to be reasonable limits.

When I was a new administrator, I asked a lot of veteran leaders for advice on how to handle some difficult personnel problems. I also read all kinds of books and articles on the topic. I tried every suggestion and tip I could find. And even with that, nothing worked with a lot of the individuals. It took me a few years, but I finally figured something out: Some people lack either the will or the ability to be effective contributors to the institution and no matter what you do, you aren't going to change them.

You always do your best to do the right things to make it happen, but you cannot and should not take the blame for other adults. In the end, we are all responsible for ourselves.

The second thing I would say is that when you see a problem occur, you need to bring it to the attention of the person you are dealing with as soon as you can. You need to be clear about what is unacceptable, and why, and offer help. Some people will appreciate that, but many will not. However, and this goes back to the previous point, you can only control yourself, you cannot control others. So do the right thing and then let them decide whether they want to accept your support or not.

Here's one other observation, and it's taken a lot of years and scars to come to this conclusion: The vast majority of the time when there is dysfunction in departments, it isn't the fault of a handful of professors, but rather the fault of leadership. I know it may shock you to hear me say that, but here's my read on it: Who hired these people?

The former chair looked at her. *We did, obviously.*

The former dean nodded. *Agreed. And if we had done a comprehensive, thorough review of the candidates, do you think we would have hired all of them? I don't. I see some people getting high-visibility positions, and then the universities find out afterward that they had skeletons in their closets or they were highly ineffective or disliked in their previous jobs. Some were even guilty of serious crimes and fired, and no one knew about it until after they were hired at the next place.*

All of this is based on the failure of human resource departments and administrators or search committees to do background checks the way they should have. Nothing replaces good vetting of candidates. Interviews, essays, referrals, and providing sample lectures are all helpful. But nothing replaces thorough background checks.

Former Chair: *I have to admit, I've seen this happen too. And the worst part is that some of those people who were brought into administrative positions also were given tenure in a department so that if they were unsuccessful, they had a safety net. They stayed on in a professor role after being fired from leadership. And that was really uncomfortable for a lot of people!*

Former Dean: *Exactly.*

Let me give you some other examples. We have had plenty of conversations about the way department members typically have the major say in hiring their chairs. These same chairs are then charged with overseeing professors who will vote on their retention after a couple of years.

Many universities have made chair positions administrative appointments. This often provides better protections and benefits, and as a result they are able to draw better pools of candidates. Some do not make them administrators, but their evaluations and appointments are not dependent on the department but on their deans. This too provides a little more security to chairs that are sometimes asked to make the right decisions rather than the most popular decisions.

The last thing I'd say is this. Most colleges are made up of multiple departments. You and I have discussed the lack of staff development for people going into higher education leadership. Most schools fail to provide a concerted, consistent opportunity for new leaders to receive training in things like higher education law, supervision, program management, budgeting, and conflict resolution, just to name a few.

Universities need to be looking at new hires in the professoriate and consider whether these same candidates have the tools to someday take leadership roles in the academy. They need to provide them with mini-internships with chairs and deans and people in the central office so they can get an idea of the rewards and challenges of leading in the academy. And these can't just be one-shot deals—they need to be ongoing and institutionalized.

Former Chair: *Some good stuff here. We should sit down and write all this down to share with others.*

Former Dean: *Great idea. This might make a good book!*

FIFTEEN

Suggestions

"What lies behind us and what lies before us are tiny matters compared to what lies within us."

—Ralph Waldo Emerson

Throughout this book the fluidity of individuals moving across the Axis of Negative Behaviors, and the uniqueness of individual needs, was repeated a number of times in various scenarios. There is a good reason for this. Quite simply, humans are complex characters. Making assumptions or trying to anticipate an individual's responses to certain actions is a fool's errand. Assuming that the same remedy will be successful when applied to two different individuals in similar situations is highly unlikely.

While leadership is part science, it is also, to a great degree, art. Leaders can certainly learn through textbooks and classes, but experience, observation, instinct, and trial and error share an equal if not more important role in the success of any effective individual.

At the same time, people in leadership are faced with making, quite literally, hundreds of decisions on a daily basis. It is almost impossible to have all of the facts and data on hand before making every decision. As a result, one thing leaders need to learn to do is know when they have an adequate amount of information at hand in order to make what they hope will be the correct calls.

As stories were gathered in preparing to write this book, the three categories of behaviors provided by the Axis emerged along with the stories in each of the cases: Passive, Passive-Aggressive, and Aggressive. Complementing them were the personality types that helped describe the faculty members that were introduced: Resistors, Reluctants, and Committed. And finally, references were made to the common psychological needs of fun (enjoyment), power (control), and love (affiliation).

The individuals in the case studies regularly crossed the Axis as well as the personality types. However, it seems in life as in this book, people lean toward one place on the Axis as well as one personality type more than the others. Likewise, while we may all have psychological needs in common, the amount we require of each will vary depending on our backgrounds, our lives both inside and outside of our professions, and a myriad number of other complex, individual factors.

With all that in mind, it seemed appropriate to summarize some ideas about how to respond to our Committed, Resistor, and Reluctant faculty. This list is certainly not conclusive. A number of suggestions were shared within the text. In addition, those reading this will undoubtedly have observed and witnessed approaches in their own lives that they can add to it.

SUGGESTIONS FOR SUPPORTING COMMITTED FACULTY:

1. Make sure they know why they are so valued. Point out how important their ability is to helping establish future stability. Thank them . . . often.
2. Provide them leadership opportunities with minimal supervision. Stay in touch, but don't smother.
3. Ask Committed faculty to help deal with meaningful initiatives that need to be addressed.
4. Involve them in training opportunities. Their role in changing the culture will be necessary and developing their skills to do this will be helpful.
5. For those who would be interested, give them opportunities to use their skills and knowledge in areas outside of the college that might involve them in activities such as grants, special programs, and teaching in other departments.
6. Provide internships that will expose them to leadership activities in the chair's and dean's offices; allow them time to meet and observe central office administrators. Give them a chance to talk to sitting administrators about how to "climb the ladder" in administration.
7. Start all new hires on the leadership track before you hire them. Ask about their potential interest in leading initiatives, as well as possibly being a chair or dean later in their careers. Groom those who have an interest once they have become established in their roles as instructors.
8. Work with central administration in providing leadership workshops for faculty (as well as staff members who may have an interest in pursuing other opportunities).

SUGGESTIONS FOR SUPPORTING RELUCTANTS:

1. Develop personal relationships with Reluctants as soon as they are hired. Their first impressions will be critical to their long-term perceptions of the department as a workplace.
2. Institute a "Buddy-Professor" system. Assign a new hire to a positive, effective veteran professor immediately. That person will act as a "Big Brother" or "Big Sister." They are someone that the new hire can call and get help from with mundane day-to-day concerns, as well as more important career advancement questions.
3. If the Reluctant is not a new hire, look for opportunities to have him or her team-teach or work on joint projects with other highly effective faculty members.
4. Develop peer-group meetings for Reluctants (as well as others who might be interested) in learning more about working in a university setting. Give them others to lean on and share with.
5. Be protective of Reluctants and new hires. Keep the dean and provost well-informed of sensitive situations that may occur. Make sure Reluctants know that they can be assured of fair consideration for their work.
6. Put notes in your calendar to touch base with them regularly to see how they are doing.
7. Have the department personnel committee and their Buddy-Professor provide trainings in how to assemble the dossiers they will compile for consideration for reappointment and tenure.
8. Find them opportunities to gain experiences they can add to their resumes such as co-writing articles or grants, involvement in conferences, and serving on committees.
9. Look for things Reluctants do right to build their confidence. Recognize them in newsletters, with letters of commendation, and with a pat on the back whenever such praise is earned. Be specific when you communicate with them about what they did right, and let them know how their contribution will support the department's mission.

SOME IDEAS FOR DEALING WITH RESISTORS:

1. Deal with issues immediately. If you don't, they will only continue to persist and get uglier. Provide constructive feedback and suggestions.
2. Deal with facts. Be transparent. Where appropriate, include others in the conversations. Rumor and innuendo are often the friends of Resistors; facts and data the enemies.

3. Remember that Resistors are people too. Many want to be productive, but do not know how. Always start out with a helping hand. Try to understand what psychological or safety needs they might have that are not being met and try to respond to them.
4. Offer opportunities to better satisfy needs that may not be getting met: different courses to teach, staff development, leaves of absence, team-teaching, and if possible, retirement or part-time options.
5. Always engage in face-to-face conversations when discussing difficult matters. Many Resistors are bullies and enjoy stirring up drama from afar.
6. Capitalize on resources at your disposal, such as the union or a colleague of the Resistor. If a Resistor sees you as the enemy simply because you have a title such as chair or dean before your name, it can be helpful to ask someone they trust to point out a problem. Work with colleagues and union representatives, if it is practical to do so.

About the Author

Rick Castallo is a professor of educational administration at California State University Northridge. During his tenure at CSUN he spent seven years chairing two different departments in the College of Education. Prior to that, he spent nineteen years coordinating the Educational Administration Program at the State University of New York at Cortland, and was also an elementary, middle school, and high school teacher; and spent seven years as a secondary school assistant principal and principal.

A number of Dr. Castallo's publications have appeared in discipline-related journals. Books he has authored include *School Personnel Administration* (Allyn and Bacon), *Focused Leadership: How to Improve Student Achievement* (Scarecrow Education), and *Focused Leadership: School Boards and Superintendents Working Together* (Scarecrow Education).

Castallo has been a speaker and consultant to hundreds of school boards and administrative groups focusing on building more effective leadership teams.

Made in the USA
Middletown, DE
24 March 2021

36157459R00099